ROUTLEDGE LIBRARY EDITIONS: PSYCHOANALYSIS

Volume 1

UNCONSCIOUS CONTRACTS

UNCONSCIOUS CONTRACTS
A Psychoanalytical Theory of Society

MICHAEL ALLINGHAM

LONDON AND NEW YORK

First published in 1987 by Routledge & Kegan Paul Ltd

This edition first published in 2016
by Routledge
2 Park Square, Milton Park, Abingdon, Oxon OX14 4RN

and by Routledge
711 Third Avenue, New York, NY 10017

Routledge is an imprint of the Taylor & Francis Group, an informa business

© 1987 Michael Allingham

All rights reserved. No part of this book may be reprinted or reproduced or utilised in any form or by any electronic, mechanical, or other means, now known or hereafter invented, including photocopying and recording, or in any information storage or retrieval system, without permission in writing from the publishers.

Trademark notice: Product or corporate names may be trademarks or registered trademarks, and are used only for identification and explanation without intent to infringe.

British Library Cataloguing in Publication Data
A catalogue record for this book is available from the British Library

ISBN: 978-1-138-93453-5 (Set)
ISBN: 978-1-315-65239-9 (Set) (ebk)
ISBN: 978-1-138-93446-7 (Volume 1) (hbk)
ISBN: 978-1-138-93879-3 (Volume 1) (pbk)
ISBN: 978-1-315-67793-4 (Volume 1) (ebk)

Publisher's Note
The publisher has gone to great lengths to ensure the quality of this reprint but points out that some imperfections in the original copies may be apparent.

Disclaimer
The publisher has made every effort to trace copyright holders and would welcome correspondence from those they have been unable to trace.

Unconscious Contracts

A PSYCHOANALYTICAL THEORY OF SOCIETY

Michael Allingham

Routledge & Kegan Paul
London and New York

First published in 1987 by
Routledge & Kegan Paul Ltd
11 New Fetter Lane, London EC4P 4EE

Published in the USA by
Routledge & Kegan Paul Inc.
in association with Methuen Inc.
29 West 35th Street, New York, NY 10001

Set in Century
by Inforum Ltd.
and printed in Great Britain
by T.J. Press Ltd.,
Padstow, Cornwall

© Michael Allingham 1987

No part of this book may be reproduced in
any form without permission from the publisher
except for the quotation of brief passages
in criticism

Library of Congress Cataloging in Publication Data
Allingham, Michael.
  Unconscious contracts.

  Bibliography: p.
  Includes index.
  1. Sociology. 2. Psychoanalysis. I. Title.
HM27.A44   1987   301   87-4973

British Library CIP Data also available
ISBN 0-7102-0996-7

Contents

Preface vii

CHAPTER 1
The structure of society 1

CHAPTER 2
The individual mind 11

CHAPTER 3
Individual development 33

CHAPTER 4
Individuals and the group 48

CHAPTER 5
Groups and society 74

CHAPTER 6
Social attitudes 106

Notes 129

Index 135

Preface

This book was conceived during the years when I was both an associate at the Tavistock Clinic in London and a professor of social science at the University of Kent. Its subject matter reflects this personal splitting and, I hope, integration. It has one root in psychoanalysis and one in social science: from the two I attempt to grow a unified and fruitful tree.

The subject matter, with its emphasis on unconscious processes, falls within the ambit neither of what is generally known as social psychology nor of what is generally known as sociology. If it falls within any generally recognized rubric at all it is probably that of 'applied psychoanalysis'. Being concerned with the unconscious the material of psychoanalysis cannot, when it is unacceptable to our conscious minds, be dismissed simply because it seems patent nonsense. By the same token it cannot, when it proves more acceptable, be justified simply because it seems obviously true. The rejection or acceptance of ideas about the unconscious can only be made, gradually and tentatively, as the whole picture of their implications is built up. I would then invite the reader to suspend judgment as the theory unfolds until a more complete picture of its implications emerges.

Enquiries into the workings of our minds are controversial enough; and those into the social implications of our deepest phantasies even more so. My aim in this book is not to present a critical analysis of the various ways of thinking about the

PREFACE

problem: it is simply to develop one such way in depth, and to explore some of its implications. Any comparison and evaluation I leave to the reader.

Some of the material of the book has been read at scientific meetings at the clinic, and some delivered as lectures at the university. I also draw on two previous works: *Value*, and a paper in *The Journal of the Melanie Klein Society*.

I am grateful to all those who have made this work possible: the clinic for providing a stimulating working environment, the university for its generous financial support, my editor at Routledge & Kegan Paul and his readers for their encouragement and suggestions, and all those who have helped by discussing the subject matter and commenting on the manuscript. But my main gratitude is to John Denford for fostering the learning from experience which gave birth to this book.

CHAPTER 1

The structure of society

Adam Smith laid the foundation stone of social science in 1776 with his famous (or infamous) creation of the invisible hand. 'He intends only his own gain, and he is . . . led by an invisible hand to promote an end which was no part of his intention . . . . By pursuing his own interest he frequently promotes that of society more effectually than when he really intends to promote it.'[1] Over a century and a half later Sigmund Freud had found the keystone of his psychoanalytical interpretation of society. 'The meaning of the evolution of civilization is no longer obscure to us: it must present the struggle between Eros and Death, between the instinct of life and the instinct of destruction, as it works itself out in the human species.'[2]

These are two brilliant and bold conjectures. Smith's has received a wealth of attention over the last two centuries, some supportive and some critical: whether accepted or not, it is at least well understood. Freud's conjecture has received less rigorous attention, and what it has received has taken little account of Smith's. My purpose in this book is to explore the extent to which psychoanalysis and social science, the paradigms of Sigmund Freud and Adam Smith, can together generate a more rigorous psychoanalytical theory of society – to explore how the nature and institutions of society depend on the underlying, and typically unconscious, aims of its members. The key to this will be the interpretation of both psychoanalysis and social science in terms of the interplay between conflict and co-operation, whether conscious or otherwise.

Consider a couple of familiar observations. The message of Jesus is love. 'Love the Lord your God . . . ; Love your neighbour as yourself; Everything in the law and the prophets hangs on these two commandments.'[3] Yet organized Christianity has given us, along with love and creation, much hatred and destruction: holy wars; the persecution, and even extermination, of religious minorities; and so forth. The main aims of the democracies of the world are to provide their subjects with both freedom and the satisfaction of their material wants. Yet such systems have given us, along with liberty and prosperity, much needless control and deprivation: civilians are conscripted into peacetime armies; mountains of food are stored, or even destroyed, while people go hungry; and so forth.

There is nothing novel in these observations, but they are none the less true, or important, for that. In each case ordinary people are joined together in some sort of contract, albeit unconsciously, to produce an extra-ordinary social outcome. At the same time as our overt aims are co-ordinated by Adam Smith's dextrous invisible hand, our more hidden desires, the hatred which accompanies the love, or indeed the hidden love which accompanies the hatred, are guided by another, sinistral, invisible hand. It is the workings of this sinistral invisible hand, through the medium of unconscious contracts, which I explore in this book.

The examples I have given are extreme. The social outcomes are not consciously desired by anyone: the persecuting Christian is no more satisfied than his or her[4] victim; and both farmers and the hungry could benefit by not destroying food. But the unconscious contracts of society also produce a variety of other social outcomes, or institutions, which, although less dramatic, have a profound and pervasive effect on our lives – both for good and for ill. We organize ourselves into families, classes and nations; we satisfy much of our material needs through the division of labour by working together in firms; and we raise armies to fight wars with somewhat vague aims but quite formal ground rules.

The twin premises of the exploration which I undertake in this

THE STRUCTURE OF SOCIETY

book are that social arrangements may be seen as contracts involving the various members of society, and that such contracts are, at least in part, unconscious. By the first premise I do not mean that each individual explicitly subscribes to the contract, but rather that what happens in a society, given the available options, can only be a function of the aims of its members. To put this premise another way, there is no external organizing force for society: if God intervenes in His creation then He does so only through His creatures.

By the second premise I simply mean that the unconscious motives which influence our lives as individuals and our relations with those close to us also influence our wider social relations. Almost every night each of us dreams; we laugh at jokes; and we sometimes make 'intentional errors'. We fall in love for reasons which may only become clear much later, if at all. All of these are manifestations of unconscious processes. If they affect our private lives so pervasively they may also be expected to have some effect on our social lives.

Since psychoanalysis is, in Freud's words, 'the science of unconscious mental processes',[5] the exploration of unconscious contracts may be interpreted as an attempt to construct a psychoanalytical theory of society, that is to say, a coherent general explanation of the institutions adopted by society in terms of the underlying aims of its members. Accordingly, I shall not be directly concerned with any particular social institutions, such as organized Christianity or political democracies, though I shall draw on these as specific examples of the general theme.

In the remainder of this chapter I shall spell out the question I am asking in a little more detail, and at the same time compare the approach I take with that adopted by Freud. In chapters 2 and 3 I summarize the more relevant aspects of the working and the development of the individual mind, that is, the mainstream of psychoanalysis. As will become apparent, the group is an essential link between the individual and society: in chapter 4 I explore the behaviour of individuals in groups and the sense in which groups have lives of their own. The core of the theory is contained in chapter 5, in which I explore how the behaviour, both conflicting and co-operative, of the various groups in society

THE STRUCTURE OF SOCIETY

determines the nature and institutions of society itself. The development thus far is general in that it does not depend on what the particular aims of the members of society may be. In the final chapter, chapter 6, I return to these aims, and examine the unconscious motives which underlie our conscious social and political aims.

In a strict sense, society may be taken to comprise the totality of the human species – the whole of mankind. No man is an iland, intire of it selfe. Even the hermit is bound to the rest of society by the very forces which keep him apart: indeed, his life is dominated by the need to stay away from his fellows.

However, it is also useful to use the term society more loosely, and as an approximation, to refer to any collection of individuals which is, at least in some respect, effectively self-contained. Whether or not a particular collection of individuals is effectively self-contained, that is to say how good the approximation is, will depend on the context. Thus for some purpose we may reasonably consider a nation as a society, while for others, such as the nature of war, this would be absurd. Similarly, in some contexts, but not others, we may reasonably treat a social class, or even a family, as a society.

I am concerned with society's institutional arrangements, that is to say, with the ways in which it 'organizes' itself and 'agrees' on various customs and rules. Of course, much of this activity is at an implicit or even unconscious level, so the 'organization' may appear to be most disorganized and the 'agreement' fraught with overt disagreement. But, consciously or otherwise, societies do organize themselves and agree on rules. They arrange for their material well-being through the institution of the market, or some alternative to this; they raise armies and wage war on one another; and they satisfy their spiritual needs by congregating in churches, whether of the overtly religious variety or otherwise. It is arrangements, or institutions, such as these that I shall be concerned with.

Freud, in *The Future of an Illusion*,[6] saw civilization or culture as consisting of those aspects of human life which distinguish it from that of the beasts. He saw these aspects as falling into two categories. The first of these is technology, that is, all the capacities which man has acquired in controlling nature and extracting its wealth; the second is the institutional structure, that is, all the regulations governing the relations of men to one another, and especially the distribution of wealth provided by technology. Although he sometimes equates the two he tends to reserve the term civilization (*Zivilisation*) for the former and culture (*Kultur*) for the second. Freud's categorization makes it clear that technology and institutions are not independent of one another since institutions are concerned, among other things, with distributing the wealth made available by technology. But this categorization also makes it clear that it is quite legitimate to look at society at some point of time, with its given technology, and enquire why it has adopted the institutions it has. This is the approach I follow.

Although this approach is less ambitious than Freud's it is still potentially important. In *Civilization and its Discontents*[7] Freud sees human ills as arising from three sources: the power of nature, the fragility of the body and the inadequacy of our institutions. The first two of these are aspects of technology, pure or medical, which must be taken as given: we must live today with the realities of the physical world as it is. But the third of Freud's ills, the inadequacy of our institutions, is open to change: within the constraints of our physical environment we may do as we choose. This is not to suggest that the problem of the inadequacy of our institutions is trivial. Mankind has not organized itself spectacularly successfully for the last ten millennia, let alone the last century, and there is no reason to suppose that it will change overnight. But the possibility of improvement exists, and an understanding of how institutional arrangements are arrived at may help bring this about.

Not only is this enquiry less ambitious than Freud's in that it only concerns institutions and not technology, but also, and indeed as a result of this, it is less ambitious in another respect. Freud is concerned with the evolution of civilization over time, from our humble beginnings in the primal horde, as he saw them, to our flowering, or wilting, in modern capitalism. Thus Freud's approach is essentially historical, or dynamic. The approach taken here, on the other hand, is timeless. We are looking at society as in a still photograph, and explaining what we see.

This explanation is of some importance in that no progress can be made on the dynamic question until the timeless question is answered. In the language of systems theory, we may see the unfolding of the historical drama in the following terms: the state of the system (that is, the institutions of society) yesterday determines the parameters of the system (that is, the aims of the members of society and its technology) today; today's parameters then determine today's state; today's state determines tomorrow's parameters; and so forth. I am concerned with the basic link of how today's parameters determine today's state.

There is a parallel between this distinction between the timeless and the dynamic and Saussure's distinction, originally applied to linguistics, between the synchronic and the diachronic. Pre-Saussurian linguistics was essentially historical: languages were investigated primarily with a view to exposing their parents and earlier ancestors. Saussure, however, emphasized the importance of language as a state as it is, in the here and now: 'The linguist who wishes to understand a state must discard all knowledge of everything that produced it, since what produced it is not part of the state.'[8] This change of emphasis from the diachronic to the synchronic, which in linguistics gave birth to modern structuralism, has its counterpart in our investigation. Freud, as Kermode notes,[9] took an essentially diachronic view of society — and also, in so far as he alluded to the subject, of linguistics. Not unnaturally, post-Freudian social theory has tended to follow in his footsteps. In contrast, I shall be more concerned with the synchronic problem.

I am concerned with the ways in which the nature and institutions of society depend on the underlying aims of its members. Since, as will become clear, consciousness is simply the visible tip of the iceberg, these underlying aims will typically be unconscious; I shall therefore concentrate on unconscious aims. This is not to deny the importance of conscious aims. In some cases conscious aims will simply be underlying aims made conscious:

for example, an underlying desire for feeding may be expressed as a conscious desire for food. In such cases considering the underlying aim is effectively the same as considering the conscious aim. But in other cases conscious aims will be acceptable distortions of unacceptable underlying, and still unconscious, aims: to take an example which I consider later, a conscious desire for equality *may* be a distortion of an underlying and unconscious desire to spoil and destroy. In these cases considering the underlying aim requires concentrating on the unconscious aim; the conscious aim will still be relevant, but as a symptom rather than a cause.

It is important to distinguish between the unconscious aims in the minds of the various individuals in society and those of the 'collective unconscious' of society itself. The approach I follow will involve only the aims of the individual members of society, and have no recourse to any concept of a collective unconscious. There are two reasons for this. Firstly, the existence, and indeed to some extent the workings, of the individual unconscious mind may be demonstrated in a variety of ways: dreams, jokes, 'intentional errors' and so forth. But the existence, and even the meaning, of a collective unconscious is far from clear. Secondly, even if the concept of a collective mind were to be acceptable an explanation based on more primitive elements, that is, the various individual unconscious minds, would be more powerful. The position is analogous to our understanding of radio waves: theories which involve the concept of ether give us some explanation, but whether or not ether exists the modern theory of electromagnetism provides a far more powerful, useful and elegant explanation.

Freud, in *Totem and Taboo*,[10] his first systematic study of society, did make use of the concept of a collective mind, though uneasily. He was aware that his thesis depended on the existence of a collective mind with the same mental processes as the individual mind, and in particular a sense of guilt persisting for thousands of years. Freud acknowledged that there were grave difficulties with this, and that an explanation which could avoid the concept of a collective mind would be preferable. It is worth noting, however, that Freud was writing before he developed his final instinct theory (the theory of the life and death instincts, which was to form the core of his thinking of civilization), and also before his break with Jung – indeed, in his preface Freud specifically acknowledged his debt to Jung's social psychology.[11]

After Freud had developed his final instinct theory, and after his break with Jung, he effectively abandoned the concept of a collective mind. In *Group Psychology*[12] he interprets his subject matter as being concerned with the individual as a member of a group, and suggests that the social instinct is not primitive but explicable in terms of individuals' family and emotional origins – a position Freud later confirms in one of his encyclopaedia articles.[13] Towards the end of his life, in *Moses and Monotheism*,[14] Freud returns to the thesis of *Totem and Taboo* but now accepts that little is to be gained by introducing the concept of a collective mind.

The development of Freud's work may, among other ways, be categorized as following one of two directions: a deepening and a broadening. The first of these, which forms one of the strands of mainstream psychoanalysis, is the deeper penetration into the world of infantile experience of the Kleinian school. Although Melanie Klein herself wrote little directly on society, the Kleinian school has been fertile in this field, and has almost wholly followed Freud's later position in eschewing any concept of a collective mind. For example, Bion, with his wide experience of collective phenomena, never encountered any which required the concept of a collective mind for their explanation.[15]

The second direction, which lies outside the mainstream of psychoanalysis, is the broadening out into individuals' cultural and social environment of the so-called neo-Freudian school. This school does make use of the concept of a collective mind, though not wholeheartedly; perhaps its main concern is with what it sees as an excessively individualistic emphasis in the work of Freud. Thus Fromm, one of the original neo-Freudians, criticizes Freud on explicitly Marxist lines, pointing out (quite correctly) that Freud sees human relations as similar to the economic relations which characterize the individual in capitalist society, with each person motivated entirely by his own drives.[16] But even Fromm rejects sociological theories which reduce individual psychology to a shadow of cultural patterns;[17] and Marx himself clearly rejected the concept of society as an abstraction in relation to the individual.[18]

There is a basic difference between an explanation of social institutions based on a collective unconscious and one based on unconscious individual aims. This is that the former needs only what I shall call a behavioural theory, while the latter needs both a (different) behavioural theory and what I shall call an aggregation theory. A collective unconscious approach needs only an explanation of how society as a whole behaves in various circumstances and responds to various stimuli (a behavioural theory); it needs nothing further. On the other hand, an individual unconscious approach needs a corresponding explanation of how individuals behave and respond (an individual behavioural theory), but this is not enough. It also needs an explanation of how the behaviour of the various individuals in society, sometimes in conflict and sometimes in co-operation, determines the nature and institutions of society – that is to say, an explanation of how individuals' behaviour is combined (an aggregation theory). The social theories of Freud and his followers differ in many ways, but they have one aspect in common: any aggregation theory is at best only implicit – and often absent entirely.

As I have noted, a collective unconscious approach needs no aggregation theory. For example, Freud's thesis in the final essay of *Totem and Taboo*[19] is that the original form of society was that of Darwin's primal horde with a powerful male keeping the other males under his absolute control and the females for his own gratification; this state of affairs persisted until the subjugated males killed and devoured the leader and possessed the females. The unconscious memory of this primal crime, in the form of guilt and defences against its re-occurrence, is used to explain a wide range of social phenomena, particularly the incest taboo. Whether this story is convincing or not, it stands on its own: it needs no explanation of how any conflicting aims might be reconciled, since everyone suffers the same guilt for the primal crime.

On the other hand, an individual unconscious approach does

THE STRUCTURE OF SOCIETY

need an aggregation theory; if this is lacking, or only implicit, any explanation will be incomplete. For example, one of Freud's basic themes in *The Future of an Illusion*[20] is that the entire edifice of civilization is based on the renunciation of instinctual pleasure, since civilization is built by work rather than by erotic gratification. This renunciation of pleasure is achieved only through coercion, so we experience one part of society, indeed the smaller part, coercing the other, larger part. This results not only in a loss of gratification by the majority, but also in a similar loss by the minority. It is only natural to ask why the majority does not resist the minority, or even coerce the minority into accepting instinctual pleasure so that the combined power of erotic ties prevails and civilization crumbles. An answer to this question would be an aggregation theory; without this the whole story may prove to be valuable or it may not, but it will be seriously incomplete.

I may now re-state my purpose a little more precisely. This is to explain the institutions of society in terms of the underlying, and typically unconscious, aims of the various individuals in society, taking the technology and history of society as given. This requires both an individual behavioural theory and an aggregation theory. I now turn to the former, and in particular to the workings of the individual mind.

CHAPTER 2

The individual mind

The workings of the individual mind may be approached from two perspectives: the static and the developmental. The static approach, which I pursue in this chapter, investigates how the mind operates at some given stage of development, that is, taking all the individual's past, all his memories, and all the ways of functioning which he has learnt, as given.

The developmental approach, on the other hand, investigates how the past affects the present – how the child is father to the man. Basic to psychoanalysis is the premise that as we develop from infancy onwards we never completely forget the ways of functioning which we have learnt earlier, and particularly the ways which we learnt first of all, as infants. Thus the most mature adult carries with him, quite unconsciously, ways of functioning and relating to people which are essentially infantile. To understand these ways we must return to the world of the infant. Although these two approaches cannot be separated completely it is helpful to explore them one at a time. I shall therefore postpone the discussion of individual development until the next chapter.

As I propose to use the fruits of this investigation of the individual mind only for the study of society I shall concentrate on the ways in which the workings of the mind affect, and are affected by, the nature of the individual's, or subject's, relations

THE INDIVIDUAL MIND

with those around him, that is, with his objects: how he loves, how he hates, and how he may do both at the same time.[1]

As we cannot observe the mind itself we shall need, as a frame of reference, a model of the mind, in the same way as we need a map to understand the layout of some unfamiliar terrain. The purpose of a map is to give us an overview, a sense of perspective. It is not to overwhelm us with detail: a map with a scale of one-to-one is of little use. Not only will a map simplify, by omitting unimportant details, but also it will distort, by quite deliberately enlarging important aspects: if roads were not widened on large-scale maps they would scarcely be visible to the naked eye. In just the same way a model of the mind will both simplify and distort.

We do of course require some consistency in the model. Firstly, it must be internally consistent, that is to say, it must stand as a logical whole; and secondly, it must, broadly speaking, be externally consistent, that it to say, it must accord with what we can infer, albeit indirectly, about the workings of the mind. Thus we do not ask whether the model is true or false; all we ask is that it be consistent, and useful.

I shall start by looking at the model as a whole, identifying the various components and examining how these fit together. Only when this is done will I consider the components of the model in any detail. This gives us an immediate sense of purpose and direction, albeit at the cost of having to accept, for the time being, some ill-defined and unexplained concepts.

The processes of the mind originate in the instincts: drives seeking satisfaction in objects. Accordingly, the processes terminate in these objects. We may thus think of the mind as the apparatus which relates instincts to their objects, or which mediates between the internal reality of instincts and the external reality of objects. The mind is, as it were, the connector in the sentence 'I love you'; 'love' is the instinct, 'you' the object, and 'I', that is my mind, the mediator between the two. Schematically, we may think of the mind, in the simplest possible terms, as represented in Figure 2.1.

This diagram emphasizes that the mind is a process, that is,

THE INDIVIDUAL MIND

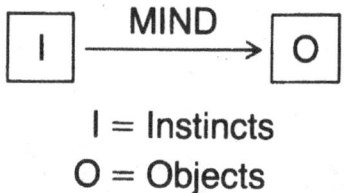

I = Instincts
O = Objects

Figure 2.1

something which transforms inputs (instincts) into outputs (objects, or, more accurately, relations with objects) – rather as a refinery transforms copper ore into ingots. But the mind is a complex process, and it is useful to think of it as the product of various components – just as a refinery first transforms ore into blister by milling and smelting, and then transforms blister into ingots either by firing or by electrolysis.

The primary process of the mind relates instincts to phantasies, or unconscious ideas, and the secondary process relates phantasies to objects. The primary process (the analogue of milling and smelting) is relatively simple, but the secondary process may follow one of two routes: either a direct phantasy route (the analogue of firing); or an indirect reality route through thoughts (the analogue of electrolysis).

The secondary process, which is the seeing and partly conscious part of the mind, is, not unnaturally, referred to as the ego, or personal 'I'. The primary process, which is the blind and wholly unconscious part, is, less naturally, referred to as the id, or impersonal 'it'. As this structure implies, and this is a basic premise of psychoanalysis, only part of the mind is conscious. Strictly speaking, it is only thoughts which are conscious, but by extension I shall also refer to external objects, and to relations between thoughts and objects, as conscious. Everything else in the mind is unconscious. A slightly more detailed picture of the mind now emerges: this is represented in Figure 2.2.

As this diagram makes clear, the model involves components of various types. Firstly, there are the processes, or structures, of the mind, that is, the id and the ego – these are represented by arrows. (Strictly speaking, these alone comprise the mind.) Secondly, there are the ideas generated in, or contents of, the

THE INDIVIDUAL MIND

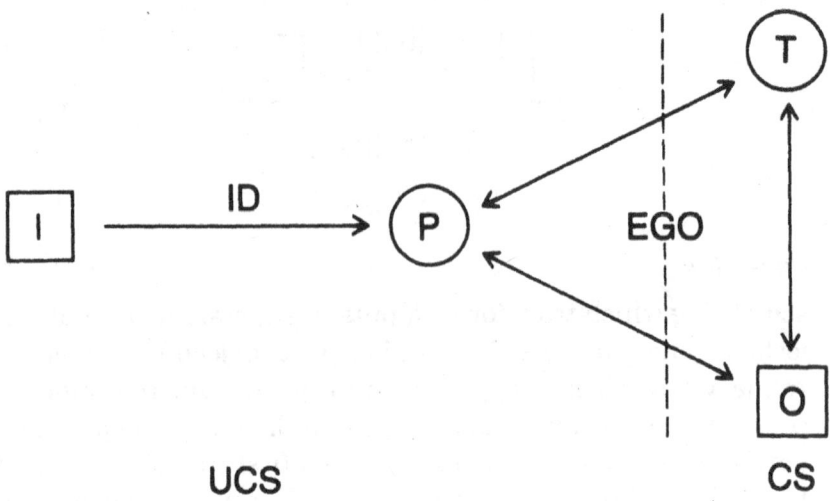

I = Instincts   O = Objects   P = Phantasies   T = Thoughts
Figure 2.2

mind, that is, phantasies and thoughts – represented by circles. And thirdly, there are the data, or parameters, of the mind, that is, instincts and objects – represented by boxes. The basic distinction between conscious and unconscious (in its extended sense) applies across these: objects, thoughts and some parts of the ego are conscious; instincts, phantasies, the id and the remainder of the ego are unconscious.

In discussing the individual components of the model I shall start with an examination of the basic distinction between conscious and unconscious; this, in essence, reduces to that between thoughts and phantasies. I shall next consider the parameters, that is, instincts and objects, and only then turn to the processes of the mind itself, the ego and the id. This is not the most logical order of approach, but, as in the sentence 'I love you', the logical order is not always the most direct.

Ideas are states of mind: feelings, desires, memories, beliefs and so forth. Thoughts are simply conscious ideas, that is, ideas I am aware of: I may feel hungry, desire to eat, remember yesterday's dinner, and believe the shop is open today. As well as ideas which

THE INDIVIDUAL MIND

I am immediately aware of there are other ideas which I can recall to awareness or consciousness at will: I can remember how to make bread. I shall consider as conscious, and thus as thoughts, both ideas which I am immediately aware of (sometimes referred to as conscious proper) and those which I can bring to my awareness at will (sometimes referred to as preconscious). As this discussion makes clear, thoughts are not just the products of purposeful thinking (indeed, as we shall see, thoughts lead to thinking rather than vice versa). However, a basic property of thoughts is that they do have some sort of order – if only in that they can be put into words, at least to some extent.

Strictly speaking, we can only be aware of ideas, not of objects: when I speak of being aware of a lover I mean that I am aware of the idea of the lover in my mind. None the less, I shall consider objects which are represented by conscious ideas, that is, by thoughts, as being conscious, as well as relations between thoughts and objects. Consciousness is a basic fact of experience. I shall take it as understood, and offer no definition or further explanation.

Phantasies are unconscious ideas, that is, all ideas I am unaware of, or all ideas other than thoughts. Phantasies are not the same as fantasies, in the sense of whimsical speculations. They are more primitive and less reasonable than such speculations, much closer mental representations of instincts. They are expressed, or rather experienced, directly rather than symbolically or verbally. If they are put into words as accurately as possible they may, if taken literally, seem to be nonsense – as the (manifest) contents of dreams often do. For example, behind my desire to eat may lie unconscious memories of being nourished as an infant at the breast together with the desire to repeat this experience. (This example, as any example, is somewhat misleading since by expressing the phantasy in words we necessarily change its basic nature and make it more, if not completely, reasonable.)

By definition, we have no direct evidence for the existence of unconscious ideas, but we do have a wealth of indirect or circumstantial evidence from which we may infer both the existence, and much about the nature of, the unconscious. Perhaps the most familiar evidence is presented to each of us almost every night, in the form of dreams – Freud's 'royal road to a knowledge of the unconscious'.[2] But we also have the evidence of humour, 'intentional errors', creativity, psychosomatic symtoms and much more. This mass of evidence makes it clear that there is more to the mind than consciousness; the unconscious is simply that which remains.

Closely related to the basic premise of the existence of the unconscious is the principle of mental continuity: that apparently unconnected thoughts are in fact connected, in the sense that unconscious ideas fill in the gaps between conscious ones. It is as if we are flying over mountainous terrain in low cloud: all we see are mountain peaks, appearing and disappearing as our journey progresses, and as the cloud level changes, apparently at random. But if we could peer through the cloud cover we would see the whole pattern of hills and valleys which would explain, at least to some extent, the apparently arbitrary disposition of mountain peaks. Thus, for example, while watching an old film I may, apparently without reason, remember to buy a birthday present for my father. What I do not see, what is unconscious, is that the ambience of the film reminds me of my infantile love for my mother, of guilt for the wish to oust my father, and of the desire to make some reparation.

The principle of mental continuity, or determinism, need not be understood in the extreme sense. It may well be that there are genuinely random psychic events just as there are physical ones, such as Brownian motion. The principle remains useful if it allows us to explain any apparently unexplainable phenomena. In the same way, the division between conscious and unconscious is neither fixed nor absolute; ideas may move from being conscious to unconscious and vice versa (as we shall see), and some ideas, such as daydreams, linger on the border. The cloud level may rise or fall, and we can always see a little into the first few feet of cloud.

I turn now to the parameters of the mind, that is, to instincts and their objects. Instincts and their objects are closely connected in

THE INDIVIDUAL MIND

that instincts are drives directed towards objects, and objects are only significant if they are the targets of instincts. Thus objects are not 'things', but rather targets. Indeed, because instincts involve relating to objects and relating requires at least the possibility of some mutual involvement, objects are essentially other people, or at least aspects or parts of them.

As we shall see, the infant's first objects are his mother's breast (as part of the mother), then his whole mother, his immediate family (and particularly his father in relation to his mother), and only then more distant people. But first objects, and memories of them, always remain important, as does the device of representing objects by their parts. Thus the adult man may marry a woman who unconsciously reminds him of his mother, and at least some of his internal images of his spouse may be as parts – her face, breasts, and so forth; and, of course, the adult woman may behave in a corresponding fashion.

Instincts, as I have stressed, are innate drives directed towards objects. Thus they are not the automatic reflexes to stimuli manifest in all animal behaviour, but are essentially purposeful. Although instincts are directed towards objects they are actually satisfied in ideas in the mind, that is, in thoughts or phantasies, rather than in the external object. For example, a loving instinct may find satisfaction in the idea of sexual fusion with the object: not in the sense of a daydream, but as a mental or internal representation of this fusion, a representation which will typically be achieved only through actual intercourse. In this example the separation of the internal idea from the external action seems artificial, but this is not always the case. A hating instinct may find satisfaction in the idea of the enemy's death, but there may be no need to witness this event, and indeed it would be impossible to experience it. The distinction is useful in that it allows us to understand how instincts can achieve some, albeit compromise, satisfaction in symbolic acts which appear to be far removed from the direct expression of instincts, such as political, and indeed much of social, activity.

Just as instincts achieve satisfaction in ideas (thoughts and phantasies), so they are given concrete form in ideas: the instinct of 'loving' is given a mental expression in the idea (phantasy) of

THE INDIVIDUAL MIND

'love'. Instincts themselves are best seen as organizing principles, the analogues of the principles of attraction and repulsion in physics.

As this analogy suggests, there is a basic dualism between the instincts. Physical equilibrium is maintained in matter by the dynamic balancing of the dual forces of attraction and repulsion. In the same way mental equilibrium is maintained by the balance of two basic instincts. One way to characterize these is as the instinct to combine and create, referred to as the life instinct, and the instinct to divide and destroy, referred to as the death instinct.

As well as being analogous to the dual forces of attraction and repulsion which govern inorganic matter, the life and death instincts are also the analogues of the forces of anabolism and catabolism which govern organic life, and (more significantly, as we shall see) the analogues of the forces of co-operation and conflict which govern the affairs of society. However, these analogies should not be taken too far. In particular, there is a basic asymmetry between the life and death instincts: the life instinct is a positive driving force, and the death instinct a negative force which interferes with it.

It should be stressed that these apparently somewhat mythical forces are to be interpreted only as organizing principles. They only take any recognizable form when transformed into phantasies by the id, that is, roughly speaking, into love and hate. It is no accident that most literature, both 'serious' and, more significantly, 'popular', is concerned with the eternal themes of love (including sexuality) and hatred (as expressed in war or in crime).

Each instinct has both inward-looking and outward-looking aspects. The life instinct, or love, embraces both the inward-looking aspect of self-preservation and the outward-looking one of sexuality (which is why it is also known as Eros) – though self-preservation extends to the preservation of one's loved objects and sexuality includes narcissism. Similarly, the death instinct, or hate, embraces both the inward-looking aspect of wanting to return in peace to the inorganic state (dust to dust, earth to earth, ashes to ashes) and the outward-looking one of

THE INDIVIDUAL MIND

aggression – though again the two are not completely distinct.

The process which gives instincts some form by transforming them into impulses (or primitive phantasy desires), that is to say, the id, has two important properties. Firstly, out of the two polar instincts the id produces a wide range of impulses extending from something close to pure creation at one extreme to something close to pure destruction at the other. We seldom, if ever, experience impulses at either extreme: most experience is somewhere between the two, that is, involves both instincts. Sexual love is close to one end of the spectrum, but this always involves some destructive derivations, however repressed – most vernacular words for intercourse are also used aggressively. And war is close to the other end of the spectrum, but even war involves some libidinal elements – the comradeship of soldiers in their common plight, under whatever flag. Nearer the centre of the spectrum we have the perversions of sado-masochism as prime examples; but we also have more 'normal' activities such as sport, which combines some intimacy with the opponent with the desire to defeat him.

What lies at the root of love, man's central preoccupation, has exercised peoples' minds since time immemorial. One way to view this question is to see love as achieving ecstasy through the perfect fusion of the life and death instincts. A true coming together, or creation, necessarily involves some loss or destruction, albeit through transcendence, of the parties involved: the lover loses part of himself in the loved. This is just as true of agape as it is of Eros: the true believer loses part of himself in God just as much as the more earthly lover loses part of himself in his partner. It is not surprising that this fusion, at one and the same time of the self with the object, and of the two polar instincts with each other, is man's greatest preoccupation and achievement.

The second important property of the id is that it transforms instincts into impulses directly, that is, with no regard for either reason or reality. It seeks blind and immediate gratification of instincts, operating according to what is known as the pleasure principle (an unfortunate term as instinctual gratification may

THE INDIVIDUAL MIND

also involve pain, as in masochism). The id ignores external reality because, as Figure 2.2 shows, it has no way of communicating with the outer world. It ignores reason not in the sense that it lacks any order at all, but rather that it does not conform to the logic of the conscious. In particular, opposites can co-exist, and there is no sense of time. The infant, whose id is dominant, can both want to be fed and not want to be fed at the same time; and if he does want to be fed he finds it intolerable and incomprehensible if he is not fed immediately. This lack of reason and disregard for reality are both facets of the one-way nature of the id process: it transforms instincts into phantasies, but has no feedback from phantasies to instincts.

The id process is the primary process of the mind, relating instincts to phantasies. The secondary process, or ego, relates phantasies to objects both directly, and indirectly through thoughts. Thus, as is suggested in Figure 2.2, the ego may be seen as having three components: relations between phantasies and objects; relations between phantasies and thoughts; and relations between thoughts and objects.

Secondary processes take more account of reality than do primary, since they involve contact (directly or indirectly) with the external reality of objects, and they are more logical. Both of these properties arise from the fact that, as we shall see, all three components of the ego are two-way relations, unlike the one-way relation of the id. More succinctly, we may say that the ego follows the reality principle while the id follows the pleasure principle. Indeed, the ego grows out of the id specifically to take account of reality: not to replace the pleasure principle but to safeguard it, for example by postponing gratification until a better time and tolerating frustration in the meantime. The infant eventually learns that the desire both to be fed and not to be fed at the same time is doomed to frustration; and also that sometimes he will not be fed.

Not all ego processes are equally rooted in reality and reason. The relation between phantasies and objects is a quite primitive extension of that between instincts and phantasies; the relation between phantasies and thoughts is more developed; and that

THE INDIVIDUAL MIND

between thoughts and objects, being conscious, has all the rationality of consciousness. Thus we should not see the id and the ego processes as being completely distinct: rather, there is a hierarchy of processes in the mind, with each member of the hierarchy displaying a different degree of rationality – as we should expect, since the ego developed from the id. In discussing this hierarchy I shall start with its least rational member.

The two-way relation between phantasies and objects is a direct relation between the inner and outer worlds, one which bypasses thought. The outgoing part of this, that is, the process from phantasies to objects, is projection: the ego attributes its own feelings (or, strictly speaking, the feelings contained in its phantasies) to the object. This may be wholly constructive: I do not know what X feels, so imagine that X feels as I do. Or it may be more defensive: if my hatred of X makes me feel uncomfortable I imagine that he hates me instead, that is, project my hatred into him. The corresponding ingoing process, from objects to phantasies, is introjection: the ego takes over the object's feelings as its own. Again, this may be constructive: I do not know what to feel, so follow X's example. Or again it may be defensive: if I am incapable of love I may let X love me and thus believe that I love X, that is, introject X's love and take it for mine.

These twin processes may be understood more clearly if we accept that in phantasy the boundary between the ego, or self, and the object are not completely clear. Then sometimes I see part of myself as being in the object: naturally the object will have my feelings (projection). And sometimes I see part of the object as being inside me: then I will have the object's feelings (introjection). Thus both projection and introjection involve some form of identification with the object, though in different ways. In projection I identify with X by making X similar to me, and in introjection I identify with X by making myself similar to X. As we shall see, it is identification, in both its forms, which holds society together.

The processes of projection and introjection, which operate simultaneously and reinforce each other, form the basis of all our learning about the world and all our relations with others. They

THE INDIVIDUAL MIND

precede thoughts and thinking, and indeed bring these about. Even when thoughts are well-developed these more primitive processes continue to operate in parallel with them. Not only are these two processes normal ways to learn about and relate to the world, but at first they are the only ways.

Quite clearly, these processes involve an element of circularity: if I project my phantasies into X and introject what I believe to be X's phantasies then I am simply receiving my own phantasies back. But the circularity is not complete: as time goes by I develop some idea of what X's, and my, feelings really are, and this information gradually modifies the projections and introjections. Thus at first projection and introjection are dominated by the subject, that is, by phantasy, but later on reality, in the form of the object, exerts an increasing influence. Over time phantasies tend to become closer to reality, although the two seldom coincide completely. This development does not only occur as the infant makes his first relationships: it is repeated in adulthood each time a new relationship is entered. Both in infancy and in adulthood it is completely unconscious. I may be conscious of the result of projections and introjections, of 'X hating me', but I am never conscious of the process generating this idea.

Related to these processes between phantasies and objects is a process which transforms one phantasy into another (or others). This process (which is not shown in Figure 2.2) is splitting. When instincts are transformed into impulses by the id the resulting impulse may contain elements of both the life and death instincts, causing some conflict. If I both love and hate X I may fear that my hate may destroy the X whom I love; this fear is known as depressive anxiety. Or, as my feelings and my view of X's feelings are interwoven by projection and introjection, I may fear that X's hate may destroy me; this is known as paranoid anxiety. (These anxieties arise from the death instinct interfering with the life instinct, and not vice versa – an aspect of the asymmetry of the two instincts; the need to avoid the anxiety and pain this causes is an aspect of the primacy of the life instinct.)

Paranoid and depressive anxieties are kept at bay, or defended against, by splitting the impulse which causes them into

THE INDIVIDUAL MIND

its loving (or good) and its hating (or bad) components, and simultaneously splitting the object into good and bad parts (or identifying one whole object as good and another as bad). Then the good impulses are associated with the good object and the bad impulses with the bad. Typically, the bad impulses are projected into (what becomes) the bad object to be rid of them, and the good impulses are introjected from the good object to protect them. But bad impulses may also be introjected to control them, and good impulses projected to safeguard them.

The infant resorts to splitting from birth. To avoid the conflict between both loving and hating the breast that sometimes feeds him and sometimes is absent he splits it into two parts: a good breast which he loves and a bad breast which he hates. The adult employs precisely the same device: the leaders of his own political party are good, and admired, while those of the other party are bad, and denigrated. Popular literature also relies heavily on the device of the good hero and bad villain. The essence of splitting is that a good impulse and object cannot be split off without leaving a bad, and vice versa. Thus idealization of one object (the prime minister) necessarily entails the denigration of another (the leader of the opposition) – and the greater the idealization the greater the denigration. A tale with only heroes, and no villains, would be no tale at all.

By means of these processes of splitting, projection and, particularly, introjection a rich world of inner objects, or representations in the mind (as phantasies) of external objects, is built up. In this way I may hold, as an internal object, a representation of a friend from which I may obtain support in the absence of the external friend (and do the same, including obtaining support in some sense, with an internal enemy).

Early introjections, since they are virtually all the infant has, are particularly potent, and the inner objects they create are never forgotten. These early introjections, which of necessity are of parents or parental figures, create an inner object known as the superego. (This is a confusing term, as the superego is an inner object or phantasy and thus a content of the mind, rather than a part or extension of the ego, which is a process.) The introjection of the 'good' parent creates the ideal superego, that

THE INDIVIDUAL MIND

is, a sense of ideals and positive morality – a pattern of what to do. And introjection of the 'bad' parent creates the persecutory superego, a sense of guilt and negative morality – of what not to do. What is known as conscience, then, is built up by identifying with parental figures, but, as these early relations are dominated by phantasy, more from phantasy of parents (and particularly a sense of parents' own superegos) than from the reality of parents' behaviour.

Out of these direct relations between phantasies and objects develop the indirect relations through thoughts. These naturally fall into two pairs: processes from phantasies to thoughts and vice versa on the one hand; and processes from thoughts to objects and vice versa on the other. The process from phantasies to thoughts, which is the natural starting point, is simply conception, that is, the coming into being of thoughts: I 'suddenly' think of buying a present for my father. Not all phantasies become thoughts, and those which do may do so only after some distortion. Conception is simply the natural flow downstream from the unconscious to the conscious. What makes it significant is its failures, that is, the repression and distortion of phantasies.

Repression may be one of two types. Some phantasies are never allowed to become conscious, that is, to become thoughts; the process restraining them is primary repression. But in addition, some existing thoughts are 'forgotten', or forced back to become unconscious, that is, to become phantasies; the process relegating them is secondary repression. (Although secondary repression is just as important as primary, Figure 2.2, to keep matters simple, only shows primary repression.) Repression ensures that ideas which are unacceptable, that is, unacceptable to consciousness, are made unconscious, either by forcing them back to, or by keeping them as, phantasies. When watching the film my memory of infantile love, my guilt, and my desire to make reparation are all repressed: only the thought of buying a present emerges into consciousness.

Ideas become unacceptable to consciousness if they conflict too much with other ideas. The conscious part of the mind is a relatively orderly place, and only a limited amount of chaos can be tolerated. As Figure 2.2 shows, there are three connections

THE INDIVIDUAL MIND

with phantasies: connections from instincts; from objects by the direct route, through introjections; and from objects by the indirect route, through thoughts and observations. Because conflict requires the involvement of instincts to give it any force it may therefore arise in three ways: from the incompatibility between one instinct (or, more accurately the impulse, as a phantasy, representing this instinct) and another; from that between instincts and introjections; and from that between instincts and observations.

We have already encountered the first type of conflict, that between instincts, and particularly the fear of the death instinct interfering with the life instinct. This is anxiety, or instinctual conflict. As we have seen, one way to deal with this is by splitting the good (or love) from the bad (or hate). But an alternative way is to repress one instinct or the other: the love or the hate. The second type of conflict, that between instincts and introjections, arises particularly in connection with the most important introject, or inner object, that is, the superego; for this reason such conflict is known as superego conflict. I may love X but, as X is married to Y and my superego would frown on my union with X, I repress this love. The third type of conflict, that between instincts and observations, arises when the observation of reality, in the form of the real external object, shows that the instinct is doomed to frustration; this is known as reality conflict. I may hate X, but as I rely on X for support I repress this hatred.

In these three ways that part of the ego concerned with repression mediates between the demands of the instincts, the superego and reality. Primary repression is more concerned with instinctual and superego conflicts, as these first arise in phantasies and need to be kept there. Secondary repression, on the other hand, is more concerned with reality conflict, since this first arises in thoughts and needs to be forced back into phantasy.

Closely related to repression (and conception), which mediates between phantasies and thoughts, is distortion, which (in addition to, but independently of, splitting) transforms one phantasy into another. While repression keeps unacceptable ideas out of consciousness altogether, distortion modifies unacceptable ideas in such a way that they become acceptable and thus able to be admitted to consciousness. Distortion may take various forms, but as phantasies are essentially a buffer between instincts and objects the two basic forms are the distortion of instincts and the distortion of objects. An example of the former is reversal, that is the replacing of one instinct by the other. If I cannot accept my love for X because X is forbidden to me, my unconscious admiration may be expressed as contempt: desire would be frustrated, but anger can be satisfied. An example of the second form of distortion is displacement, that is, the replacing of one object by another. If I cannot vent my anger on X, whom I depend on, I may turn it on to Y, where it will be satisfied.

Reversal is the theme of much romantic literature, where the hero's love is disguised by coldness until the final chapter. And displacement lies behind the attacking of one's subordinate instead of one's employer. However, because of the intimate connection between instincts and objects most distortion involves both instincts and objects, and is thus more complex than either simple reversal or displacement. A prime example is the perversion of sado-masochism where both the instincts (life represented by sexuality and death by pain) and the objects (the self and the partner) become confused and interchangeable.

The final stage of the indirect route between phantasies and objects consists of processes between thoughts and objects. These are the familiar conscious processes of testing and responding to reality. The outgoing component of this pair of processes is action, in the usual sense: I attack X. And the corresponding ingoing component is observation, again in the usual sense: I observe that X is angry. In that all links in a chain are of equal importance these conscious processes are just as crucial as the unconscious processes. However, I do not pursue them as, being conscious, they are immediately familiar.

Closely related to reality testing, in the form of action and observation, is the process of thinking, which transforms one thought into another. By thinking I transform the thought that X is angry into the thought that I shall avoid X. But again, thinking is a familiar activity, and I shall explore it no further – other than to note that as thinking transforms one thought into

THE INDIVIDUAL MIND

another thoughts must precede thinking rather than vice versa.

This discussion of the components of the mind has expanded the picture represented in Figure 2.2 in a number of ways. The more detailed view we have obtained is summarized schematically in Figure 2.3.

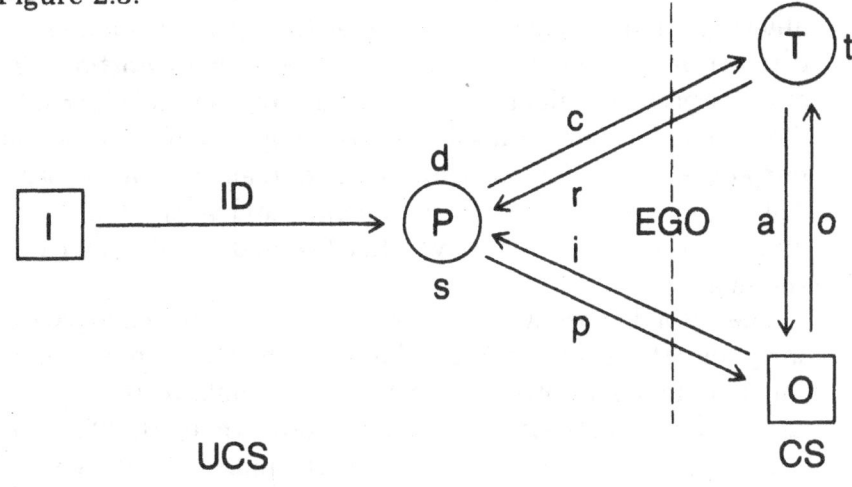

I = Instincts	O = Objects	P = Phantasies	T = Thoughts
a = Action	c = Conception	d = Distortion	i = Introjection
o = Observation	p = Projection	r = Repression	s = Splitting
t = Thinking			

Figure 2.3

The map is now quite detailed enough for our needs, though is still a simplification. However, the main way in which any such model necessarily distorts reality is not in simplification as such, but in suggesting that the various components are more separate than they really are. In fact, as we have seen, the unconscious merges with the conscious, the ego with the id, and so forth. Having then dissected the delicate tissues of the mind I shall now attempt to redress the balance and put them together again as a living organism.

There are two aspects in particular where a more holistic view of the mind is important. The first of these concerns the mechanisms of defence. Many of the processes involving the central buffer of phantasies have the common purpose of defence

THE INDIVIDUAL MIND

against conflicts (including anxiety), and so interact with one another. As conflict is more acceptable in unconscious phantasies than in conscious thoughts the central process of defence is repression – Freud's 'cornerstone on which the whole structure of psychoanalysis rests'.[3] But distortion is closely connected with this: indeed, it is hard to draw a clear distinction between not allowing an idea to become conscious (repression) and allowing it to become conscious only in a modified form (distortion). Yet another possible defence is, for example, projection, which operates in close liaison with splitting. Having as they do a common purpose, all these defensive mechanisms react with one another. The castle is not only defended by a moat and by archers, but the archers become more effective when the enemy is floundering in the moat.

The second aspect of the holism of the mind which is particularly important is the relation between the two routes connecting phantasies to objects which are available to the ego: the direct route, and the indirect route through thoughts. The direct route is the more primitive of these. The indirect route develops out of this, not to replace it but to supplement it; yet it never completely supersedes the direct, and is never completely separate from it.

The connection between the two is best understood from the process by which the indirect route grows out of the direct. The essence of this is that repeated projections and introjections (via the direct route) result not only in ideas about the object being absorbed, but also in the actual process of relating to the object being learned – that is, in learning from experience. Primitive projections are of something completely unknown, a nameless dread (this is referred to as a beta element for the very reason that the term conveys no meaning). The object, originally the mother, takes in the projections and, in a state known as reverie, transforms them (by what is known as her alpha process) into something more knowable (alpha elements), which are then re-introjected. As this process is repeated not only are alpha elements introjected, but also the alpha function itself is learned. The infant feels some unknown distress, is fed, and feels better; but as this process is repeated he receives something just as

THE INDIVIDUAL MIND

valuable as food: he receives the understanding that he is hungry. The alpha function is the basis of thoughts, and thus of the indirect route. It is as if I give a teacher a number and he tells me its square root; eventually, I learn not only the square roots of specific numbers, but also how to compute square roots myself.

This process of development requires both a rich phantasy world from which to project beta elements and into which to introject alpha elements, and also a containing object to take in the projections and transform them in reverie. Such learning from experience is the basis of all human growth and development, naturally and unconsciously in everyday life (and in a heightened way in the analytic session).

The model I have developed draws on the views of both wings of the psychoanalytic movement (the classical and the Kleinian), but in a way which attempts to integrate the two rather than reflect either faithfully. Accordingly, the meanings which I have given to various terms will not always be precisely the same as those given by particular classical or Kleinian analysts. For example, I have *defined* phantasies as being unconscious, though some analysts will refer to conscious phantasies; and, likewise, I have *defined* all conscious ideas to be thoughts, though some analysts will distinguish between conscious feelings and thoughts. It is then worth noting the differences, and similarities, between the picture developed in this chapter and the views of the classical and Kleinian schools.

Psychoanalysis, it goes without saying, originates in the work of Sigmund Freud. For its first forty years or so, when it was based in Vienna, psychoanalysis was dominated by Freud and his immediate circle. Particularly important in this circle were Karl Abraham, Ernest Jones and Sandor Ferenczi, all of whom had been in analysis, of some sort, with Freud. With the outbreak of war the centre of gravity of psychoanalysis moved to London. (On his arrival Freud revealed that 'since I first came over to England as a boy of 18 years, it became an intense wish fantasy of mine to settle in England and be an Englishman.'[4]) Coincidentally with this move the discipline started to develop in two related, though discernibly different, directions. One direction was a direct extension of the line of investigation started by Freud. This direction was pursued, particularly, by Anna Freud, Freud's daughter and analysand, who moved to London with Freud in 1938. The other area, which sought not to replace the first but to complement it by delving more deeply into its roots, developed from the work of Melanie Klein. Melanie Klein, who had been in analysis with both Ferenczi and Abraham, arrived in London in 1926. (She too had been taken with the climate, claiming that 'nowhere else but in England have I experienced this feeling of a very strong sympathy and an ability in me to adapt'.[5]) Melanie Klein had been working in the psychoanalytic society established in London by Jones for a decade or so before the direction of her work started to diverge significantly from that of Freud and his circle. Her work was extended, particularly, by Wilfred Bion, who had been in analysis with her in London.

The differences and similarities between these two directions were explored in what have come to be known as the Controversial Discussions of 1943. As a result of these discussions the society split more formally into a classical group and a Kleinian group. Those analysts who were not attached to either group formed, by default, a middle group – a group which was later to assume a more formal identity as the independent group.[6] This third group, which was numerically the largest, drew on the work of both the classical and Kleinian groups, but in a pragmatic way, developing lines of enquiry which seemed fruitful regardless of their origin. At the centre of this group were those who had been in analysis both with Freud and with Melanie Klein, and their analytical descendants.[7]

As is to be expected, Freud's views developed over his long working life; however, his newer ideas often stood beside his older without any systematic revision or integration of the two. Accordingly, Freud's later views can only be properly understood if they are taken together with his earlier.

In terms of the general framework discussed in this chapter, Freud's emphasis was on instincts, while Melanie Klein's was on objects – though it should be stressed that this emphasis was a matter of degree only, both accepting that instincts are irrelevant without objects and vice versa. Objects located in external reality are naturally interpreted in the same way in both classical and Kleinian thinking. The interpretation of instincts is, however, a little different.

Freud always saw instincts as dualistic, so that the possibility of conflict was ever present, but the nature of the dualism changed as his thoughts progressed. Originally, in the *Three Essays on the Theory of Sexuality*,[8] Freud saw the two dual instincts as being sexuality on the one hand and self-preservation, sometimes confusingly referred to as the ego-instinct, on the other. Later, mainly because of the recognition of the repetition compulsion, that is, the need to repeat unpleasant experiences, Freud saw the two instincts as the life and death instincts. In this revised view, developed in *Beyond the Pleasure Principle*,[9] the life instinct combines the two earlier instincts of sexuality and self-preservation, while the death instinct is interpreted as the desire to return to the inorganic state; aggression is seen as a distorted derivative of this desire, albeit the only visible derivative, rather than as a primary drive. Melanie Klein accepted Freud's basic dualism between the life and death instincts, but while her view of the life instinct accorded with Freud's (later) view, she saw the death instinct as aggression: a primary driving force of pure directionless destruction.

In the picture of the instincts developed in this chapter the inward-looking and outward-looking aspects of the life instincts correspond to the two components of both the classical and Kleinian life instincts, that is, to self-preservation and to sexuality respectively. And the inward-looking and outward-looking aspects of the death instinct correspond to the classical death instinct, or wanting to return to the inorganic state, and to the Kleinian death instinct, or aggression, respectively.

Freud's original view of the mind itself, that is, the connection between instincts and objects, is set out in the final chapter of *The Interpretation of Dreams*;[10] this is the topographical model, sometimes referred to as the first topography, of the unconscious and the conscious (together with the preconscious). At the same time that Freud revised his instinct theory (and, as the instincts are the driving force behind the mind, intimately connected with this revision) Freud proposed a new model of the mind. This new model, set out in *The Ego and the Id*,[11] is the structural model, sometimes referred to as the second topography, of the id and the ego (together with the superego). This new view, which was meant to augment rather than to replace the earlier view, arose mainly out of the recognition that parts of the ego, and particularly those parts concerned with repression, were unconscious; this meant that it was no longer possible to identify the repressed with the unconscious and the ego (a concept which Freud had already employed in a more general sense) with the conscious.

Melanie Klein worked within Freud's basic structure, but with a different emphasis. In terms of the picture developed in this chapter the classical and Kleinian views of the nature of the first process of the mind, that is, the id, are essentially the same. However, as regards the second process of the mind, that is, the ego, Freud emphasized the indirect route, and indeed the first leg of this: thus repression (both primary and secondary) becomes central, phantasies receive less attention, and the emphasis is on instincts rather than objects. Melanie Klein, on the other hand, emphasized the more primitive direct route, where phantasies, projection and introjection become central.

The main developments of the classical and Kleinian views may best be seen in perspective in terms of the two aspects of the holism of the mind which I have discussed above. One of the central classical developments, which stems particularly from Anna Freud's *The Ego and the Mechanisms of Defence*,[12] is the nexus of defensive processes. And one of the central Kleinian developments, which stems from Bion's *Learning from Experience*,[13] is the merging of the direct and indirect routes in the ego.

The model of the mind presented in this chapter may thus be seen as integrating the classical and Kleinian, and by extension the independent, views: it is a general or synoptic model from which the classical and Kleinian viewpoints may be obtained as special cases.

CHAPTER 3

Individual development

With the map developed in the preceding chapter as a guide I shall now trace the development of the adult personality from its earliest beginnings in infancy. As I have noted, the reason for doing this is that the first ways of relating to objects are never forgotten, nor completely replaced; indeed, as we shall see, they form the basis of our adult social and political attitudes. Accordingly, I shall concentrate on these first relations, that is, those of infancy – which occur, roughly speaking, in the first year of life.[1]

The infant's mental apparatus at birth has the general structure outlined in the preceding chapter, although of course in an immature form. The infant has instincts, and indeed without these he would die. And he has an object, his mother's breast (or substitute for this), again without which he would die. Connecting his instincts and object is his mind, that is to say, his primary id and his secondary ego. His primary unstructured id is similar to that of the adult. His ego, however, and particularly that part of his ego which emerges from learning from experience, is barely formed. But although immature, it is this ego which guides the infant's object relations, experiences anxiety and erects defences against this anxiety.

The infant's first object is the maternal breast. It is this object which provides his first, and, for some weeks, his only link with

INDIVIDUAL DEVELOPMENT

the outer world. He sees all his own bodily feelings as being due to the actions of this object, actions which may be experienced as being kind or as being cruel. Sometimes he will feel good – full, warm, comfortable, cared for – which feelings he will attribute to a good breast, which he loves. At other times he will feel bad – hungry, cold, uncomfortable, neglected – which feelings he will attribute to a bad breast, which he hates.

In this way both his instincts, of love and hate, are called into play from birth; and not only are they called into play, they are also directed at the same object. This ambivalence is the root of anxiety. The infant deals with, or rather defends against, this anxiety by the primitive mechanism of splitting. To avoid his hatred interfering with his love part of his hate is projected into the breast, so this becomes persecuting, and the remaining part is expressed as aggression against this persecutor. In a similar way, his love is projected into a good breast, with which libidinal relations are established. Thus the infant's first relations are dominated by projection, and are essentially with part-objects: the good and bad breasts as parts of the mother. But of course he does not recognize these objects as being only parts: when he is relating to the good breast this is his whole world, and similarly when he is relating to the bad.

Since the bad breast is seen as unambiguously bad, and quite distinct from the good, he suffers no 'depressive' anxiety of his own hatred destroying anything good. The main anxiety is, on the other hand, the 'paranoid' one of his bad objects destroying his good, and indeed the good parts of himself. Because of the dominance of paranoid anxiety this configuration of object relations, anxiety and defences is known as the paranoid position. (In view of the importance of splitting it is also known as the paranoid-schizoid position.) It is a configuration which will dominate the infant's life for his first three months or so. But yet it is not a stage of development which is encountered, negotiated and then left behind, albeit with some residue. It is, instead, one of the two basic modes of relating to objects which are adopted at all stages of life.

The basic defence against anxiety in the paranoid position, that is, splitting, may also be used constructively. It allows the

INDIVIDUAL DEVELOPMENT

ego to start to discern some sort of order in the world instead of chaos, and permits a certain detachment, or ability to undertake intellectual work while temporarily suspending the emotions. In the same way, the concomitant projection, and, to the extent that it occurs, introjection, are natural ways of establishing object relations – though these may also be used more defensively.

Because the ego is still immature it will typically reinforce the effects of splitting, which is intended to keep the bad from the good, by understating the bad and exaggerating the good. The first of these two reinforcements takes the form of denial – denying the existence of the bad; and the second takes the form of idealization – making the good so good and strong that it becomes safe from the bad. In extreme forms both of these inhibit development, being a turning-away from reality. But in lesser forms they too are useful: denial helps in the achievement of difficult goals, especially in war; and idealization is of the essence of being in love.

A further defence involves trying to gain control of the object, in phantasy, in an omnipotent way by getting inside the object/breast and controlling it from within. This highly aggressive form of object relations involves both projection into and identification with the object. Accordingly, it is known as projective identification – though it involves rather more than the simple combination of projection and identification.

I have somewhat loosely been treating the manifestation in phantasy of the life and death instincts as love and hate. However, these abstract organizing principles do have other manifestations: particularly important in infancy are those of greed and envy. Greed is the impulse to grab and possess all the goodness of an object, quite regardless of any possible harm to or destruction of the object. Being concerned with obtaining goodness it is thus a manifestation, albeit disturbed, of the life instinct. Envy, on the other hand, is the impulse to spoil and destroy a good object, regardless of any possible gain from or possession of its goodness. It is then a clear, and indeed first, externalization of the death instinct.

Greed and envy both arise when the infant attributes all

goodness to the good breast, particularly when this is exaggerated by idealization. At times of deprivation the infant may greedily want all that goodness now and grab more than he needs. Alternatively, he may want to be as good as the ideal breast so that he no longer has any need for it: since he cannot do this by raising himself he must do it by enviously attacking and diminishing the object. The first struggle between the life and death instincts, in the shape of greed and envy, which is fought out in the first three months of life, has a profound effect on all later personality development. To take but one example in the social sphere, it has an important bearing on political attitudes, as we shall see.

In the paranoid position the infant does not suffer from paranoid anxiety continually. His feelings of anxiety fluctuate in phase with his feelings of being cherished or abandoned. However, these feelings arise at least as much from the re-introjection of his own projections into the object as from reality. Thus a prerequisite for a predominance of good over bad feelings is a suitably containing object, that is, a mother (or mother-figure) who can in reverie transform the infant's beta elements into alpha elements. If such a container is to hand then the gradual domination of good over bad feelings gives strength to the good and, eventually, leads to a lessening of fear of the bad and thus a reduction of anxiety. As a result, the good and bad no longer need to be kept as separate, and integration begins.

The essence of this process is that the integration of the object, or of the mother, and the integration of the ego, or of the infant, proceed side by side and reinforce one another. The infant begins to realize that it is the same he that both loves and hates the same mother – who comprises both the good and the bad breasts. By this process the infant's object relations gradually develop from being essentially part-oriented to being concerned with the whole object: the mother who has both good and bad aspects.

Now that the object is experienced as being more balanced the paranoid anxiety of it destroying the infant fades. In its place, however, arises the depressive anxiety of the infant's own hatred having destroyed, and perhaps still destroying, the object

INDIVIDUAL DEVELOPMENT

he loves and depends on. He has loved X and hated Y, but now finds that X and Y are in fact the same: naturally enough, he fears that his hatred, which he hoped would destroy the bad Y, has destroyed the good X – as X and Y are one and the same. Because of the dominance of such depressive anxiety this configuration of object relations, anxieties and defences is known as the depressive position. Again this is to be seen as a mode of relating to objects which may be resorted to any time, rather than a stage to be passed through. The depressive position will be central to the infant's emotional life for the remainder of his first year.

In the depressive position introjection becomes more important. This is both because the infant starts to recognize his dependence on his mother and so tries to internalize her to possess her the more securely, and also because the need for projection decreases. With this gradual change of emphasis from projection to introjection the infant starts to develop new feelings: particularly mourning for the good breast which is feared as lost forever, and guilt for having destroyed it. It is important that these new feelings of mourning and guilt, although painful, be accepted. If they are not then the infant may sink into a state of deadness and depression. The natural emotions of mourning and guilt are then alternatives to, rather than manifestations of, depression.

If the pain of mourning and guilt becomes too great then extra defences are brought in to protect the ego. These defences, all of an omnipotent and manic nature, involve denying the dependence on the object. Typically, such defences take the form of a mixture of triumph, that is, denying the power of the object, and contempt, that is, denying the importance and value of the object. The problem with these defences is that they stand in the way of experiencing the emotions of mourning and guilt. When they weaken, as they inevitably must from time to time, they leave only depression, instead of sadness. Excessive dependence on these defences thus results in the so-called manic-depressive character: the crying clown or the life-and-soul of the party.

If omnipotent defences are not relied on excessively, so that mourning and guilt are experienced, the infant takes more positive steps to restore his injured loved object. He makes reparations both in phantasy and in reality; that is to say, he increases both his loving feelings and his loving actions. Provided that the mother continues to be present, and particularly continues to re-appear after necessary absences, the infant starts to believe that his reparations really have restored her.

This genuine reparation is to be distinguished from manic reparation, which is an alternative to omnipotence as a way of avoiding mourning. Manic reparation attempts to restore the object without feeling any guilt. This is typically achieved by ensuring that although the object is seen as being injured it is not seen as having been injured by oneself, and, because it is injured, seeing it as being inferior – as in some forms of 'charitable' giving to the 'feckless' poor. The dominance either of omnipotence or of manic reparation as a defence against mourning and guilt has a significant effect on later personality development, including political attitudes, as we shall see.

The paranoid and depressive positions originally encountered in the first year of life are at the root of all subsequent object relations; indeed, emotional life may be seen as a continual oscillation between these two positions. It is then worth summarizing their main features. The paranoid position is characterized by splitting and projection, paranoid anxiety and part-object relations; the depressive position, on the other hand, is characterized by integration and introjection, depressive anxiety and whole-object relations. While the infant's relations with the mother are dominated by projection in the first position and introjection in the second, the mother's relations with the infant are, of course, the mirror image of these. Thus the paranoid position is worked through by the predominance of good introjections from the mother – or, more simply, by being loved; and the depressive position is worked through by the predominance of good projections into the mother – or by loving.

Although the adult continually reverts to the paranoid and depressive positions quite naturally in everyday life, this process is heightened in the analytic session. I shall therefore use two

INDIVIDUAL DEVELOPMENT

examples from analytical material to illustrate these positions. In each case I shall present some brief background material, report a dream and some associations to this, and then consider some interpretations which illustrate the relevant mechanisms.

I shall illustrate the paranoid position with a fragment of the analysis of a middle-aged male lawyer with Hanna Segal.[2] The lawyer is not particularly adept at managing his practice and his clients. In particular, he is frequently late for appointments with clients because he allows the preceding client to over-run his time, though he is never late because of preoccupations of his own. More generally, he feels that he never does anything for his own benefit, but that some clients always interfere with his duty to others. Despite this, he has recently achieved some professional success in connection with some delinquents, though privately he feels somewhat ashamed of this.

He dreams that his office is invaded by a crowd of delinquents, smoking heavily, making a mess and demanding his attention. He suddenly remembers that he has an appointment with a client, and manages to get rid of the delinquents just in time. But then his wife appears and tells him that she has kept his appointment with his analyst in his place because she realized that he could not get rid of the delinquents, see his clients and arrive at analysis on time.

In recounting this dream he notes feeling depressed by the greedy and slovenly behaviour of the smoking delinquents, which he sees as representing his own greed; however, it is noticeable that he does not connect their heavy smoking with the heavy smoking of his analyst.

The dream is interpreted as relating to the analyst. The patient's object, that is, the analyst, is split into the good analyst to whom he wants to go for analysis, and the bad smokers who interfere with this aim. (Indeed, the split is maintained so rigidly that he sees no connection between the smokers and the analyst.) This splitting of the object is accompanied by a corresponding splitting of the ego, into the good lawyer who wants to see his client and the bad who, being unacceptable, is projected into the analyst/smokers who prevent this. This process of splitting allows him to retain his good feelings, as a good lawyer, while projecting his bad feelings into the figure of the analyst/smokers. At the root of this splitting is the paranoid anxiety that the bad parts of his self/object will destroy the good: the smokers will prevent both his seeing his client and his seeing his analyst. In this one quite ordinary dream we have all the central characteristics of the paranoid position: splitting, projection, paranoid anxiety and part-object relations.

I shall illustrate the depressive position with some material from the analysis of an adult woman, also with Hanna Segal.[3] The patient is relatively stable emotionally, but has some worries about her financial difficulties, and particularly the possibility of these forcing her to abandon her analysis.

She dreams of an endless sea of icebergs: she knows that they are very deep, and that the cold mountains she can see are only a small part of the whole.

Before recounting the dream she has complained of the analyst's waiting-room being poorly heated. She then associates the deep icebergs with depression – a deep pit with no warmth or feelings. They also remind her of the white wavy hair of an elderly friend who has been kind to her but whom she has neglected of late, for which neglect she feels quite guilty. Further, the rows of icebergs remind her both of rows of teeth and of frozen breasts. Finally, she remembers that she did in fact encounter her elderly friend at a meeting yesterday and offered her tea; but the friend declined, saying that she preferred coffee. She felt that her friend was somewhat distant, but comforted herself with the thought that she, the friend, was preoccupied with the recent death of her son-in-law.

The icebergs are interpreted as representing the cold waiting-room: the possibility of her not being able to pay the analyst has impoverished and exhausted the analyst, so that she too becomes an iceberg. At the same time this possibility is unconsciously experienced by the patient as a greedy biting attack on the analyst's breast, and introjected as ice in the patient's soul. Her inability to restore the analyst, who is represented by the elderly friend, after these attacks brings out feelings of depression: the white abyss. She makes an attempt at reparation, but this is refused; and when it is she tries to deny this refusal. In this dream, then, we have all the central characteristics of the depressive position: depressive anxiety, introjection, guilt and mourning.

A more broadly based illustration of the workings of the paranoid and depressive positions, and the continual interplay between these, is provided by the various crises of later life. For much of the time life proceeds apparently smoothly, with a reasonable balance between paranoid and depressive anxieties and their defences. But at certain times anxieties become particularly strong, and we regress more deeply to either paranoid or depressive functioning. Such times are known as crises, in the sense of fundamental change rather than of disaster. Crises arise when established ways of relating to objects and defences against anxiety are no longer adequate and so are abandoned, leading to a state of temporary confusion and disintegration before new and more appropriate ways of relating can take their place. Crises then are essentially healthy: if there is no disintegration there can be no progress.

Much of the workings of the paranoid and depressive positions respectively are exposed particularly clearly in two of the more important crises of later life: adolescence, and what has come to be known as the mid-life crisis.

Adolescence is brought about, or at least brought to a head, by puberty, that is, by the change to an adult body and particularly to adult genital sexuality. Adolescence involves the mind catching up with this change, or replacing the modes of object relations of childhood with the now more appropriate ones of adulthood.

The dominant anxiety of the adolescent is the unconscious fear that he remains as vulnerable and dependent as he was when he was a child. In other words, he fears that bad objects, either external or the projections of his own new and powerful adult hostilities, may destroy him and his loved objects. This paranoid anxiety may be defended against by splitting, and reinforcing the split with denial and idealization. Thus heroes of popular culture, or good causes, become unambiguously good

INDIVIDUAL DEVELOPMENT

while parents, or other generations or groups, are seen as useless, incompetent and irrelevant.

The adolescent crisis is worked through with the help of the mature love of parents, or parent-substitutes such as teachers, that is to say, love which is able to contain the split-off and projected hostility of the adolescent. If the crisis is not resolved the adolescent may succumb to schizophrenic illness or anorexia.

The mid-life crisis, to use Jaques's term, is brought about by a recognition that life is finite, that 'youth and childhood are past and gone ... death lies beyond'.[4] Early adulthood, that is the period between adolescence and the mid-life crisis, is dominated by activity: the development of sexual relations, career, family and so forth. While necessary, such activity also serves the purpose of a manic defence against badness, destruction and death; the mid-life crisis involves the acceptance of destruction, of the death instinct and ultimately of death itself.

The dominant anxiety of mid-life is the depressive anxiety of loss – of youth, opportunities and half of life. This may be defended against by manic activities such as triumph and contempt. For the crisis to be resolved lost youth must be properly mourned, and destruction and death accepted. This is fostered by mature loving, accepting both the loved object and oneself as a whole person: not perfect but with both good and destructive parts. (In many cases it can be further fostered by providing mature love for one's adolescent children – as a happy counterpart to their own adolescent crises.) If the depressive anxiety of mid-life is not come to terms with the result is either depression itself, as the alternative to mourning, or even stronger defences, manic activity and general shallowness of character.

The adolescent crisis is thus essentially a re-experiencing of the paranoid position and the mid-life crisis that of the depressive position – though of course there are also some depressive elements to adolescence and paranoid elements to mid-life. The adolescent crisis involves paranoid anxiety, splitting and part-object relations while the mid-life crisis involves depressive anxiety, integration and whole-object relations: the former is worked through by being loved, and the latter by loving. Indeed, there is a further duality: the adolescent crisis erupts because of the increasing force of the life instinct through emerging sexuality, and the mid-life crisis because of that of the death instinct through the recognition of mortality.

We return from these detours through adolescence and mid-life to find the infant, having negotiated the paranoid and depressive positions, soon to face the first real crisis of his life. He now sees his mother as a whole object, distinct from his father. But his perceptions of his parents are still highly coloured by projections of his own desires, and accordingly he sees his parents, in phantasy, as being continually engaged with each other in some as yet barely understood form of intercourse. This makes him feel hurt and jealous as they are experienced as giving each other precisely the attention and gratification which he wants for himself. He defends against these painful feelings by splitting. He sees one parent as good, whom he loves and who loves him. He sees the other as bad, and projects his own aggression into this bad parent, who is consequently experienced as a persecutor. These emerging feelings of triangular rivalry are the first stirrings of the Oedipus crisis – the familiar backbone of classical psychoanalysis.

At this stage the infant's bodily gratifications and resulting phantasies, that is to say, his sexual organization, is predominantly oral: libidinal satisfaction come from sucking and destructive satisfaction from biting. But now, as the infant grows into a child, the breast becomes relatively less important to him and a more genital sexual organization begins to develop alongside the oral one. As we might expect, the later sexual organization never completely replaces the earlier one: kissing and sucking remain an integral part of normal adult sexual intercourse. Indeed, the similarities between the infant's oral gratification and the adult's genital gratification are striking. This is not a specifically psychoanalytical observation: for example, Havelock Ellis, writing in 1900, drew the following parallel.[5]

The erectile nipple corresponds to the erect penis, the eager watery mouth of the infant to the moist and throbbing vagina, the vitally albuminous milk to the vitally albuminous semen: The complete

INDIVIDUAL DEVELOPMENT

mutual satisfaction, physical and psychic, of mother and child, in the transfer from one to the other of a precious organized fluid, is the one true physiological analogy to the relationship of a man and a woman at the climax of the sexual act.

The development of a more genital sexual organization signals the arrival of the Oedipus crisis proper: a complex of powerful and contradictory loving and hostile feelings towards both parents. At the heart of this complex of feelings lies, in phantasy, sexual desire for the opposite-sex parent and rivalry with the same-sex parent, the latter in turn leading to the fear of retaliation from this parent. But at the same time it also involves feelings of love for the same-sex parent, and of resentment of the opposite-sex parent for not abandoning its partner in favour of the child.

One particularly important aspect of the Oedipus crisis is that at this stage male and female become, for the first time, emotionally different. The boy has to adapt to a triangular situation with his original loved object, his mother, unchanged, while the girl has to adapt to a triangular situation at the same time as transferring her primary libidinal attachment from her mother to her father. Thus in developing an adult sexual relationship the boy has to transfer his feelings directly from the mother to the lover, while the girl has to transfer hers indirectly – from the mother through the father to the lover; both paths are strewn with potential pitfalls, but the pitfalls are not at all the same. The effect of this difference is that post-Oedipal male and female psychology will not be identical. (It is, of course, these differences which make male–female unions potentially so deeply satisfying.)

The Oedipus complex is significant in that its resolution, or lack of resolution, has a profound effect on the ways in which the adult will later react in his relations with the opposite sex and with the same sex, and particularly with parental figures of the same sex. By extension, it will also influence his social attitudes, as we shall see later. On the other hand, it does not involve any essentially new ways of relating: it is met with a combination of already available paranoid and depressive techniques. We may see the essence of the personality as being laid down in infancy

INDIVIDUAL DEVELOPMENT

with the learning of paranoid and depressive techniques, and the Oedipus complex as the first major testing ground of these.

This interpretation of the Oedipus complex is consistent with the background of the myth of Oedipus. As Bettelheim has pointed out,[6] Freud assumed his reader to be familiar with the whole of this myth, not just with its dramatic conclusion. The story starts in Oedipus' infancy, when he is mistreated and abandoned by his real parents, Laius and Jocasta, the king and queen of Thebes. In their place Oedipus is brought up lovingly by the king and queen of Corinth. But Oedipus does not know that this loved couple are not his real parents, so when told by the oracle that he will kill his father and marry his mother he immediately leaves Corinth to protect them. Thus when he fulfills the prophecy, killing Laius and marrying Jocasta, he does so unconsciously in the fullest sense: *he does not know* that they are his parents. (Freud therefore alludes to this particular myth to emphasize that the loving and hostile feelings towards parents are essentially unconscious.)

The turning point in Oedipus' story, when he changes from the lost wanderer to the confident king, is his encounter with the sphinx. This mythical creature is half enticing woman and half destroying beast – half good breast and half bad breast. The first part is the projection of loving feelings towards his parents, and the second that of hostile feelings. But, in projection and in reality, both are parts of the same whole: the woman and beast are parts of the same sphinx, and Oedipus' mother/wife and father/victim are parts of the same parental couple. It is only through dealing with the sphinx, which is to say dealing with his own ambivalent paranoid and depressive feelings, that Oedipus is able to resolve his own crisis – his particular resolution being so extreme because of the extreme nature of his infancy.

As I have noted, the infant, then the child and then the adult, in a process of constant development, builds up his own internal phantasy world as his inner representation of the external world of reality; this is achieved through the continual interplay between projection and introjection. Even in the most normal of people the match between phantasy and reality, or more accurately between inner and outer reality, will not be perfect. We may, unconsciously, experience paranoid anxiety even though there is no real threat from outside, and experience depressive anxiety even when we have done no real harm. Major discrepancies between phantasy and reality are known as psychotic, so that paranoid and depressive anxieties are sometimes referred to generically as psychotic anxieties.

As we all have some discrepancies between phantasy and reality we all have psychotic parts. Usually these remain dormant, but at other times they intrude, to a greater or lesser extent, on our functioning. For example, in times of crisis psychotic anxieties become overwhelming, and we regress more intensely to primitive paranoid and depressive mechanisms. More positively, activities such as being in love and primitive forms of creativity stem from these psychotic parts. What both these activities involve at root is communication, and psychotic communication, although remarkably unstable, can be extremely deep and direct.

It is important to distinguish between psychotic, or infantile, anxieties and mechanisms on the one hand and psychosis itself, or madness, on the other. Psychotic mechanisms operate within a general balance between internal and external reality. In psychosis itself the psychotic parts of the personality take over and phantasy becomes completely divorced from reality: thus the madman does not understand what he is doing.

When we face psychotic anxiety, whether paranoid or depressive, we defend against this in various ways. But such defences are never completely successful. They divert the primary anxiety into a more acceptable form rather than stemming it altogether: if a dam is not to overflow there must be a bypass channel. For example, the child's fear of retaliation from the same-sex parent for his love of the opposite-sex parent in the Oedipus crisis may be defended against by a complete turning away from sexuality. But the underlying libidinal, or sexual, instinct still remains, and will be expressed in some indirect or compromise way. This may be entirely harmless, and even beneficial to society, as it is when it is expressed in creativity, professionally caring for others, or religion. Or it may be harmful, at least to the subject if not to others, as it is when it is expressed in obsession, phobia or illness. All such compromise symptoms are, in the most general sense, neuroses (hence Freud's view of religion as 'the universal obsessional neurosis of humanity'[7]), though in a more usual sense the term is reserved for those symptoms which are experienced as being harmful to the subject.

Thus the difference between psychosis and neurosis is, in principle at least, one of quality rather than degree. Psychosis involves a breakdown of reality testing, so that the person is not aware of anything being wrong. Neurosis, on the other hand, leaves reality testing relatively unimpaired, with the result that the subject knows that his behaviour is unreasonable and that he is distressed. But the two are not unconnected, in that neurotic symptoms arise out of defence against psychotic anxieties. Thus neurosis may be seen as a defence against psychosis.

I have discussed psychosis and neurosis not because I want to suggest that society is effectively governed by pathological psychotics and neurotics, but because we all have some psychotic and neurotic parts, and these become relatively more significant when we are relating to others – which relations are, of course, the elements of the structure of society. To explore these elements further I now move from emphasizing the individual alone or with his single object to the individual as a member of a group.

CHAPTER 4

Individuals and the group

The role of groups is central to the understanding of the way in which society's institutions reflect individuals' underlying aims: the group is the key link between the individual and society. There are two aspects of this. Firstly, there is the simple fact that individuals as individuals have very little, if any, influence on social institutions. What influence they do have is typically through the groups, such as firms, trade unions, political parties and churches, to which they belong: even leaders of such groups, who may appear to be extremely powerful, only exert influence through the power of the group. The second aspect is that, in some sense, groups have a life of their own. This does not mean that they have a collective unconscious of the same nature as that of the individual mind, but rather that all individuals in a group lose some of their individual identity and merge into the group.[1]

This distinction between the 'mind' of the group and the minds of its members is of the same nature as the distinction between the class and its members in Russell's theory of types.[2] This postulates a basic discontinuity between the class and its members (or between the group and its component individuals), that is, treats them as ideas at different levels of abstraction, or of different logical types. (Russell uses this distinction to extricate himself from the well-known Russell paradox concerning sets which have themselves as elements.)

INDIVIDUALS AND THE GROUP

By a group I mean a collection of people who, on certain matters, act together. In this connection acting together does not mean acting in harmony or co-operatively at the conscious level: it may well mean acting together in some form of conscious conflict, albeit with some unconscious co-operation. I have mentioned firms, trade unions, political parties and churches: all of these groups can be seen as acting together on some matters, yet fighting within themselves on others. Other examples on the larger scale are nations, social classes and so forth. All Englishmen, both capitalist and worker, may act together on some issue, such as supporting their football team or fighting an enemy nation: on another issue, however, workers of the world may unite and act together. Of course, many groups are much smaller. We have professions, families, and indeed that primitive group the sexual couple, all at times, but not all the time, acting together.

An individual cannot avoid belonging to groups: he is a member even if the tie consists in his always acting to distance himself from the rest of the group – as in the case of the hermit tied to his fellows by the need to maintain this distance. As is clear from some of the examples I have mentioned, the group need not meet physically to exist as a group: group behaviour is easier to observe if the group meets, but it goes on regardless of whether it is observed or not. Although group behaviour may seem more credible in small groups which meet than in large ones which do not, what Freud was primarily concerned with in his seminal *Group Psychology*[3] was the behaviour of masses: large numbers of people who do not usually know one another and who achieve their coherence only through accepting common ideas. As Bettelheim notes, 'mass psychology' would be a more accurate translation of the original '*Massenpsychologie*' than is 'group psychology'.[4]

Thus society can be seen as consisting of a myriad of interlocking groups, at any one time some of which will be active and some latent. An individual will belong to many groups, and will often play an active role in two or more overlapping groups at the same time. For example, a member of parliament is just that, but at the same time may be an impassioned member of his

INDIVIDUALS AND THE GROUP

party, and indeed many other groupings within, and outside, parliament. In so far as it is possible to separate the two I shall reserve the discussion of how groups relate to one another (and the idea of a latent group) for the following chapter, and concentrate here on the behaviour of an individual as a member of some particular (active) group.

It is basic to psychoanalysis that behaviour, individual or group, may be irrational in some sense yet still display some sort of order. The idea of a group having a life of its own may best be seen in this coming together of irrationality and order. In this connection it is useful to distinguish two types of rationality, which I shall call external and internal rationality. I violate external rationality if my actual external choices are inconsistent with my claimed conscious wishes: that is, if I claim to prefer X to Y but when both are available choose Y instead of X. I violate internal rationality if my conscious wishes themselves are internally inconsistent: that is, if I claim to prefer X to Y, and Y to Z, but also Z to X. Internal rationality is more fundamental than external: we may have internal rationality without external, but cannot in general have external rationality without internal.

As well as irrational behaviour I shall be concerned with volatile behaviour, that is, behaviour where wishes and choices change violently and rapidly for no apparent external reason. Even extremely volatile behaviour is not irrational, since rationality concerns configurations of wishes and choices at a point of time: even the most rational person will change from one point of time to another. But when such changes become extreme this will prove to be of interest.

The most 'normal' of individuals is irrational in the external sense quite pervasively: he makes a variety of 'deliberate mistakes' (forgetting appointments, slips of the tongue, losing things), he repeatedly places himself in distressing situations (replacing one 'unsatisfactory' partner by another who is almost identical), and so forth. The reason for this is that his actual choices are determined by his unconscious impulses, which may differ from his conscious wishes. But on the whole individuals

INDIVIDUALS AND THE GROUP

are rational in the internal sense. There may be occasional inconsistencies, but these are not pervasive. Volatility is a matter of degree: at one extreme 'normal' people (or, more accurately, people while behaving 'normally') may be quite consistent, while at the other psychotics (or the same people while behaving psychotically) may be extremely volatile.

With groups, however, the position is more complicated. Firstly, since the various individuals in the group will be irrational in the external sense, we should certainly expect the group as a whole to be irrational in this sense.

Secondly, even if all individuals in the group are rational in the internal sense the group as a whole may well be profoundly irrational in this sense. Consider, for example, a group of three (internally) rational people, say Sigmund, Melanie and Wilfred. This group is faced with three possible choices, say X, Y and Z. Sigmund prefers X to Y and Y to Z, and also of course X to Z – that is to say, he ranks the choices in the order X, Y, Z; Melanie ranks these in order Z, X, Y; and Wilfred in the order Y, Z, X. These preferences may be summarized as follows.

Individual	Ranking
Sigmund	X Y Z
Melanie	Z X Y
Wilfred	Y Z X

Assume for the time being that the group makes its choices democratically, that is, by majority rule. Then the group as a whole will claim to prefer X to Y and Y to Z, but also Z to X, so will be (internally) irrational. Now of course the group may make its choices by many mechanisms or customs other than democracy, but it is a remarkable fact (which I explore in the appendix to this chapter) that whatever mechanism the group adopts it will, in general, be irrational in this sense.

Thirdly, even the most consistent of individuals tends to become volatile, often extremely so, in a group – or, in other words, regresses from using 'normal' to using psychotic mechanisms. This idea is central to the understanding of groups which I explore in the remainder of this chapter.

INDIVIDUALS AND THE GROUP

Thus group behaviour is essentially, rather than exceptionally, irrational: the group is the mutable rank-scented many. This is not a specifically psychoanalytical observation. Le Bon, writing in 1895, characterized groups as being impulsive and changeable, credulous and lacking any critical facility, open to violent fluctuations between extremes, intolerant of doubt and completely unconcerned with truth.[5] Group irrationality is openly manifest in everyday experience, from family quarrels, to working parties which do not work, to mass fascism and communism.

As I discussed in chapter 3, the problems the infant has in relating to his first objects, namely the breast, then the whole mother, then the parental couple, are quite overwhelming to his fragile and barely formed ego. He suffers from the paranoid anxiety of being destroyed by his bad objects and the bad parts of himself, and also from the depressive anxiety of destroying the good parts of himself and his good objects. Faced with these primitive anxieties, the infant turns to the only defences he has available: the primitive ones of splitting good from bad, projection (of good parts to protect them and bad to be rid of them), and introjection (of good parts to have them and bad to control them).

The central premise of the psychoanalytical theory of groups is that the adult, when brought into emotional contact with the group (a contact, which, as we have seen, is unavoidable), unconsciously re-experiences all the primitive anxieties he first experienced as an infant making contact with his first objects; as a result, he reverts to the same primitive defences as he employed then. In other words, when faced with making contact with the group the individual regresses more completely to primitive paranoid and depressive mechanisms. This regression is both involuntary and unconscious. Also, it is not the only activity that occurs; the individual maintains some sense of his own adult identity and needs, and he also joins with the group at an adult level in working towards satisfying the needs of the group. But these unconscious infantile mechanisms always exist beside, or rather underneath, the adult activities.

Thus the life of the group at the unconscious level is dominated by paranoid and depressive anxieties. In the light of this, and the inherent irrationality of groups, it is not surprising that group behaviour can be impulsive, extreme and intolerant. I shall first explore the way in which these anxieties are manifest in the members of the group, and then examine the ways in which the group as a whole acts to reinforce individuals' defences against such anxieties.

One aspect of this unconscious regression to infantile mechanisms by individuals in a group is that we may characterize a group as being a collection of people in similar states of regression. But for this regression to take place the individuals must believe that the group exists – a belief which can thus become self-fulfilling. It is this self-fulfilling belief which gives the group a life of its own, and also its volatility.

The essential tie which holds the group together, and thus allows it to have a life of its own, is the process of identification. Each individual in the group unconsciously identifies with the leader (in a sense which I shall discuss later) of the group, and thus indirectly identifies with one another. By this process each member of the group loses some of his individual identity and becomes a real part of the group as a whole. This identification with the leader may be either through introjection or through projection, that is, through precisely those mechanisms used by the infant to make contact with his first objects. Although I shall discuss these two types of identification separately, in practice they operate simultaneously and interact with one another.

Identification with the leader by introjection involves unconsciously taking the leader, or some aspect of him, into oneself so that he becomes part of one. It would typically operate in, for example, a church, where each Christian would take a part of Christ into himself and so identify with Him; indeed, this somewhat abstract activity is given symbolic reality in the eucharist, where the communicant eats His flesh and drinks His blood.

Identification by projection involves what is essentially the reverse process, that is, unconsciously putting parts of oneself into the leader so that he is seen as having the same attributes as oneself. This would typically operate in, for example, an army, where each soldier puts part of himself into the commander, or

INDIVIDUALS AND THE GROUP

even a symbolic flag; then when the commander is killed or the flag captured the army falls into disarray: it has lost its identity with its leader.

The content of the life which the group has of its own may be expressed through the idea that all members of the group unconsciously share some 'basic assumption' about the purpose of the group, an assumption which may have little connection with the manifest purposes of the group. It is as if the basic assumptions expressed the unconscious impulses of the group while the manifest purposes expressed its conscious wishes: the former obey the laws of the primary process and the latter those of the secondary process. Alternatively, we may say that basic assumptions embody the common unconscious anxieties experienced by group members in their joint regression to primitive infantile mechanisms. If, as is often the case, the basic assumption of the group differs markedly from its manifest purposes, then the group will function badly, that is to say, will have little success in achieving its manifest purposes. This is just as is the case for an individual: if my unconscious impulses differ substantially from my conscious wishes I am unlikely to have much success in satisfying these conscious wishes.

There is a range of basic assumptions which the group may have, just as an individual may have a range of instinctual impulses. In the same way as it is useful to consider an individual's impulses as lying along a spectrum between the two polar extremes of the life and death instincts, we may see the group's basic assumptions as lying along a spectrum between two polar extremes. Some basic assumptions will be close to the first extreme (even if none coincide with it perfectly), some will be close to the second and others will be mixtures of the two.

One polar basic assumption, that of dependence, is that the group exists in order to receive goodness, support and nourishment in some way. This goodness is felt to come from outside, though may be experienced through a leader in the group. Thus the basic assumption is that the group exists to take in, that is, to introject, some external good object. An example of a group which typically operates in dependent mode (in this sense) is a church, which exists to receive goodness from God, but often through the medium of a minister, or Jesus, or even a Bible.

The second polar assumption, that of hostility, is that the group exists in order to fight, or equally to flee from, some enemy. This enemy is perceived as being outside; the function of a leader of such a group is to maintain this idea of an enemy. Thus the basic assumption is that the group exists to keep out or force out, that is, to project, some bad object. Armies typically operate in hostility mode (in this sense); they exist quite explicitly to deal with enemies and need an enemy, and also a leader who can keep the idea of an enemy alive, in order to function well.

In this context I am using the idea of a leader as the leader of the group's unconscious basic assumption activity, and not necessarily of its conscious manifest activity. The leader of the group is thus just as much a creature of the group as is any other member. His role is to act as an object for unconscious projections and introjections by other members of the group. In the dependency group individuals introject good things from outside through the leader, and in the hostility group they project bad things outside through the leader. This means that the leader need not be the member with the 'strongest personality'; on the contrary, he will typically be the member who has lost his individual identity the most, for such a person, as a blank screen, is the best vehicle for absorbing projections and allowing re-introjections. Indeed, many potent leaders are no longer even alive, and so have, in one sense, lost their individual identities completely: Jesus and Marx are two obvious examples.

The role of leader may devolve on to some individual in the group, or it may equally be filled by some external and abstract ideal. An example of an abstract leader is the history of the group, often formalized as a 'Bible'. Thus a group may make detailed records of its meetings, and subsequently appeal to these to guide or lead the group, just as courts of law rely on precedents. One of the main appeals of a Bible is that it helps to maintain the status quo and avoid change: as change often evokes unconscious anxieties its avoidance is one of the main unconscious purposes of many groups. The concept of a Bible naturally reminds us of churches, and thus of dependency groups. But the concept is to be found just as frequently in hostility groups, for example in the unnecessarily rigid and detailed instructions for performing simple tasks in an army.

It may seem that the group's basic assumption of dependence is the analogue of the individual's life instinct, and the group's basic assumption of hostility that of the individual's death instinct. Although there is some connection this would be an oversimplification: basic assumptions arise from the whole constellation of instincts, anxieties and defences, and cannot be reduced to any one of these. For example, there is also some connection between dependence and the individual's depressive mechanisms, both of which emphasize introjection, and between hostility and paranoid mechanisms, both of which emphasize projection.

It would also be an oversimplification to suggest that the basic assumption of dependence is always operative in churches, or that of hostility in armies. Dependence certainly fits naturally in churches, and hostility in armies, but both churches and armies, as all groups, may experience any basic assumption. However, the fact that one of the basic assumptions open both to churches and to armies is singularly well suited to their respective manifest purposes explains why each of these groups can, at times, be extremely powerful. As we have seen, groups tend to founder when their basic assumptions are significantly at variance with their manifest purposes. Thus churches are not particularly successful in coming to terms with change, and peacetime armies need the constant stimulus of battle, even if this is in training or exercise.

An essential aspect of basic assumption activity is that the group has only one basic assumption at a time. It may be under the sway of the basic assumption of dependence, or of hostility or indeed of some composite basic assumption, but only one of these. If it holds some composite basic assumption it holds this is as compound rather than as a mixture of its components — just as water is a compound of hydrogen and oxygen but quite distinct from either. More generally, basic assumption activity, as all primary process activity, does not recognize reason and com-

INDIVIDUALS AND THE GROUP

promise, or even time itself. A corollary to this is that the group may change from one basic assumption to another, and back again, quite capriciously – just as at a political rally a group may switch from receiving the support of its leader to fighting the opposition, and back again, almost instantaneously.

The reason why basic assumption behaviour is so volatile is that group members unconsciously participate in these common basic assumptions to defend themselves against the psychotic anxieties which are awakened in them by emotional contact with the group. But these defences, as all defences, are only partially successful: while they may help to relieve one anxiety they also tend to arouse new anxieties, which in turn lead to a new basic assumption. For example, the basic assumption that the group depends on its leader for goodness and support may, in some cases, defend against a paranoid anxiety of having insufficient goodness and nourishment; but this will also arouse unconscious feelings of envy and aggression against the leader, which in turn will arouse feelings of guilt and anxiety of harming him. These new anxieties may be defended against by displacing the aggression on to something outside the group, that is, by developing the basic assumption that the group exists to fight some external enemy.

An important example of a composite basic assumption which combines dependence and hostility is that of pairing. This basic assumption is that the group exists to promote, witness and encourage the pairing of two of its members with a view to their producing something for the group: a baby, idea, Messiah or utopian ideal. Although this obviously refers back to the primal scene with the two parents coupling to produce a child, in its revived form as a basic assumption the sex of the pair, who are the group's leaders in this sense, is immaterial. The directly sexual aspects of the pairing are forgotten, leaving only the productive aspects. This basic assumption combines both dependence and hostility in that the product of the pairing, the Messiah, will both provide goodness for the group from outside and also deliver the group from an external enemy. An obvious example of this basic assumption is in the Christology of the later gospels (particularly *John*) where the pairing of God and

Mary produces the Messiah who will both give the world the goodness and forgiveness of God, and also save it from the dark powers of evil.

We might note in passing that Bion saw pairing as an independent basic assumption in its own right rather than as a composite one, and accordingly based his view of groups on a triad of basic assumptions: dependence, hostility (which he refers to as fight-flight) and pairing.[6] Apparently quite coincidentally, Trotter, in *Instincts of the Herd*,[7] a work which, albeit in an antithetical way, influenced Freud's *Group Psychology*, proposed a similar triad. Trotter characterized group behaviour as being protective, as in the case of sheep, aggressive, as in the case of wolves, or more primitive, as in the case of bees. It is natural to associate sheep, being led by the good shepherd, with dependency; to associate wolves, snarling and marauding, with hostility; and to associate bees, coming together to make honey, with pairing.

Although the basic assumption of pairing may be held in that most primitive group, the sexual couple, it is not the only basic assumption the couple may share. The basic assumption of the couple may well be dependency, with one person (the roles often switching) being seen by both as the provider of goodness and strength. Alternatively, it may well be hostility, as in the babes-in-the-wood couple withdrawing into each other from a hostile outer world. Indeed, in the case of couples these two polar basic assumptions reflect Freud's categorization of object choice into the narcissistic and anaclitic types.[8] In narcissistic object choice the lover reminds one, quite unconsciously, of oneself; the narcissistic couple withdraw into each other just as if they shared the basic assumption of hostility. In anaclitic object choice the lover reminds one, again unconsciously, of a parental figure; the anaclitic couple lean on each other for support, just as if they shared the basic assumption of dependence. As Freud pointed out, the type of object choice one makes is not fixed: in basic assumption terms this is to say that the couple may switch from dependency (or anaclitic functioning) to hostility (or narcissistic functioning) and back again. Thus in a strict sense we should not speak of an anaclitic couple but of a couple in anaclitic mode, and so forth.

INDIVIDUALS AND THE GROUP

As I have noted, certain groups tend to be, though are not always, dominated by some specific basic assumption. This suggests that, seen from the context of the larger group of society as a whole, these subgroups have a specific purpose. This purpose is typically to contain the relevant basic assumption behaviour and so neutralize its effects in the rest of society, thus letting the rest of society proceed with its manifest activities without being overwhelmed by these basic assumption activities. This is one, but not the only, reason why people feel a need for a church to exist even though they do not worship or even profess no faith, and also why they feel a need for an army even if it is purely ceremonial and quite unfitted to fighting any real enemy. A corresponding subgroup which is used to contain the basic assumption activity of pairing, for example, is the aristocracy: hence the deep involvement, even of many republicans, in royal pairings.

The life of the group is based on the anxieties of its members, anxieties which tend to be manifest in the form of basic assumptions. But not only does the group arouse primitive anxieties in its members, it also provides a system of defences against these anxieties – or, more accurately, provides a framework which reinforces individual defences against individual anxieties.

The general way in which the group helps to alleviate individual anxieties is by sharing and externalization. Because individuals in the group have regressed to similar stages they necessarily share similar unconscious anxieties. This in itself provides some support, in the sense of a trouble shared being a trouble halved. However, the main support comes from the common externalization of the inner conflicts associated with the anxieties. In this process individuals in the group simultaneously project their internal conflicts into a subgroup, or possibly another group altogether. These conflicts can then take place at some remove, in a relatively safe way, and then be re-introjected in a more acceptable form.

Such processes are at the centre of everyday life. We may put all our hopes and fears into two teams (a good team and a bad team) at a football match: our anxiety-provoking conflicts are

INDIVIDUALS AND THE GROUP

more safely acted out on the football field than in our minds. If we do not enjoy football we may do the same with political parties instead of football teams. The general aim is to master the internal world through mastering the external. It is essentially the same process as that of the analytic session, where the analysand projects inner conflicts into the transference relation with the analyst, works through these in this relatively safe environment, and re-introjects the outcomes.

The subgroup involved in this process is involved in an active collusive sense. It co-operates with the main group in reducing that group's anxieties, and in return achieves some diminution of its own anxieties: football players and politicians alike receive fame and attention. Of course, such collusion and co-operation is unconscious: indeed, its essence may be the maintenance of conflict at the conscious level. This two-way process may be made clearer by considering separately the ways in which both paranoid and depressive anxieties are dealt with, although in practice these two anxieties exist together and interact with one another.

The paranoid anxiety of being attacked and destroyed by something bad may be defended against by projecting the bad object or impulse into some subgroup, or second group. This second group may then absorb and contain this projection directly, and thus take on the role of being bad. Alternatively, the second group may deflect this projection on to some third group, which in turn becomes bad. Indeed, an important function of large groups is to provide an array of such bad (and indeed good) roles. Individuals in the initial group benefit from this process in two ways. Firstly, their bad impulses have been shared with other members of the group, and thus in some sense purged. And secondly, when these common impulses are re-introjected they are more acceptable than they were in their raw form, as the persecutions of some bad internal object: better the (external) devil one knows than the (internal) devil one doesn't.

For example, a country may collude in projecting all its aggressive and destructive impulses into its army, seen as a subgroup. This is not so that the army becomes bad, though this may also happen, but so that the army can deflect these aggressive impulses on to some third group: the army of an enemy country. Naturally enough, this process is not without its comeback, for the enemy army will retaliate with physical counter-attacks on the first country. But these real objective attacks, however physically terrible, may be easier to bear than the phantasy attacks, often of unimaginable horror, of internal persecutors – hence the strong feelings of emotional well-being reported of London in the 1940 blitz, for example. At the same time, the army obtains some relief from the depressive anxiety and guilt which arises out of its aggressive attacks on the enemy: its own destructive impulses can be denied through the phantasy that it is simply protecting the rest of the population.

The depressive anxiety of destroying something good may be defended against more directly by protecting the good object from attacks by splitting it off from the bad and turning the attacks on to the latter. Churches, as well as many other groups (not to mention the psychoanalytic movement), do this: Christians split off from Jews, Protestants from Catholics, Anglicans from Nonconformists, and so forth. Each party to the split reinforces its belief in its own truth and goodness by denying that of the other. And, if it is able to do so, it may back up this denigration with active persecution: Jews persecuting Christians in the first century and Christians persecuting Jews in the twentieth. At the same time, the minority, by this very persecution, are relieved of some of their own unconscious guilt and depressive anxiety.

I shall illustrate the dynamics of group behaviour with three case studies. One involves a temporary and deliberately artificial institution, while the other two involve more permanent and 'real' institutions: one operating effectively as a single group and the other employing a committee as a subgroup of the main group.

The first case study is based on a group relations conference of the Tavistock model, as developed by Bion, Rice and others. The group I am concerned with consists of the forty or so members of the conference, most of whom are associated with the Tavistock Clinic, together with the conference director and his staff. This

INDIVIDUALS AND THE GROUP

group meets for some forty hours spread over five days: it is intended to be, in an almost circular sense, a 'temporary educational institution which is itself available for study'. Members meet in a variety of settings: general plenary sessions, small study groups, a large group event, and so forth. I am primarily concerned with the large group event.

The institution is deliberately artificial, in the same way as is the analytic session, in that the constraints of time and space are rigidly set out, but no direction is given as to how this time and space are to be used. An example of the rigidity of these constraints, which is to have important repercussions, occurs at the opening plenary session – essentially an introduction by the director followed by questions from the members. One question is asked just as the time set aside for the session ends: instead of answering it, the director leaves the room without making any comment whatsoever – to the general alarm of the members.

The large group commences with the conference director reminding the group of the constraints of time (some six hours) and space (four large rooms), and also of its nominal purpose, or primary task; this is the somewhat Delphic one of knowing itself, or 'studying relatedness and relationships between groups in the here and now'. The director then withdraws; no further instructions are given.

The immediate response to this *carte blanche* is a sense of panic. Members are overwhelmed by the anxieties aroused through their being in a large and apparently leaderless and directionless group. A few suggestions as to how to proceed are made, but all of these are aimed, explicitly or implicitly, at dividing the large group into smaller, more comfortable, groups in order to avoid the vulnerability and paranoid anxiety experienced in the large group. But this possibility in turn arouses depressive anxieties, for the large group now exists and to divide it is to destroy it. Thus the interplay of paranoid and depressive anxiety, and indeed of the life instinct preserving unity and the death instinct creating divisions, is experienced from the outset.

The group remains caught in the deadlock of wanting to divide but being unable to do so for some time. Discussion as to how the division might be achieved, for example on study group lines, by

INDIVIDUALS AND THE GROUP

physical proximity and so forth, is characterized by panic: one proposal will be embraced enthusiastically, only to be replaced equally enthusiastically by a quite contradictory proposal. The need is to do *something*, no matter what.

Eventually, as tension mounts, action replaces thought. A few members announce that they are leaving, and do so forthwith. They are immediately followed by some more, while others, equally decisively, indicate their intention to remain. The individual's decision, when the time comes, to leave or to stay is spontaneous and without thought: when the group does divide it does so instantaneously, as a crystal.

Following the split there is in each new group a brief honeymoon of self-congratulation from having at least done something, but this is soon followed by doubts. The leavers experience the depressive anxiety of having snubbed the stayers, and the paranoid anxiety of having burnt their boats. The stayers experience the depressive anxiety of having driven out the leavers, and the paranoid anxiety of now being vulnerable: both smaller and with a potential enemy.

The large group had given way to panic partly because it had no clear leader. The two new groups, however, apparently find themselves with leaders. That of the leavers is one of the first few to have left the large group. He is a leader for the basic assumption activity of hostility in an obvious and direct sense, having led the flight from the large group; but he is also a leader for the basic assumption activity of dependence – having led the group out of Egypt he will now feed it in the land of milk and honey. The apparent leader of the stayers, similarly, is one of the first to reject the idea of leaving. He is in a position to lead any necessary fight with the defectors, and also to act as a dependable pillar of strength and support. However, neither leader is particularly potent for, as we shall see, there is a common absent but still powerful leader of each of the new groups.

When it comes to commencing work on the primary task both the leavers and the stayers find themselves as paralysed as they did when they formed one large group. Work is inhibited by four processes.

Firstly, members feel that they cannot start working until an agenda and some ground rules are drawn up – talks about talks. Superficially, this is an appealing position, as it is easier to start working if one knows what to start on. But its real purpose, as soon becomes apparent, is to prevent work starting altogether: all the time available for work is devoted to procedure.

Secondly, any interpretive comment, that is any potential contribution to the primary task of understanding the group, is neutralized and dissolved by the group forcing it back on to the member who makes it. Thus when someone suggests that the group is paralysed by fear of its repressed destructive impulses getting out of hand he is seen as being the destructive member of the group. And when someone else suggests that in fact the group may be more frightened of its libidinal impulses getting out of hand he becomes an object for free-floating libidinal feelings. In this way the group splits destructive impulses from libidinal ones, or bad from good: the former are projected on to the member who voices them, and the latter are retained but given as their object the member who voices them.

Thirdly, members externalize the primary task and try to work on it in the other group, where it is at a safe distance. Thus there is much discussion of what the other group might be doing, whether they are doing it 'better', and so forth. This successfully avoids discussion of what the group itself is doing.

The fourth process by which work is inhibited is that of individual members temporarily leaving the room, typically when they feel frustrated by what is, or is not, happening. This hinders group work not because the individual is needed for this, but because in his absence he dominates the discussions of the group: he is felt to be deviant, phantasies of him joining the other group are aroused, and so forth. Just before the end of the event one member (in fact of the leavers group) announces that he indeed intends to join the other group: in retrospect, he is felt as having been a hidden leader of the group all the while.

Through these processes work on the primary task is avoided. Members feel that they have learnt nothing. But, of course, they have learnt something: they have learnt that groups find it difficult to get down to work – or to learn. In this way the almost circular purpose of the conference becomes justified.

INDIVIDUALS AND THE GROUP

An important interpretation of one aspect of group activity only becomes clear in the final plenary session of the conference. This is that the real leader of the large group and of both the smaller groups has been the absent conference director. He is identified with in the most direct way: by emulating his abrupt departure. All apparent group leaders, who have themselves engineered abrupt departures, have simply been containers for this abstract ideal.

The more general implications of this exercise can be seen only in retrospect. All the manifestations of group behaviour, with one exception, apparently so closely related to the personalities of the individuals in the group, have almost precise parallels in all large group events of this type. The exception, which arises from the chance occurrence of a question being asked precisely at the end of the opening plenary session, is the particular identity of the absent leader. (For example, all the events discussed by Rice in his description of the Tavistock model[9] are characterized by manifestations which are remarkably similar to those I have described.) The clear implication, and real point of this case study, is that group behaviour depends primarily on group structure and only secondarily on the personalities of the individuals in the group.

The second case study is based on Isabel Menzies's work on the functioning of a large London teaching hospital.[10] The group I am concerned with is that of the nursing staff as a whole. There are some 700 nurses in all, about a fifth of whom are fully trained and a further fifth are in each of four years of a training programme. The manifest purpose of this large group is clear: it is to care for patients and at the same time train nurses – almost all training is of the on-the-job variety. However, unconscious anxieties and their defences seriously interfere with this aim: to note but one symptom, about a third of all nurses voluntarily fail to complete their training.

The objective reality of the work of nurses – their direct involvement with suffering and death, intimate physical contact and so forth – evokes intense infantile anxieties. The immediate response to these anxieties is the defensive response of the infant: avoidance rather than confrontation. This means that

65

when nurses unconsciously project their anxieties into their work they simultaneously build up a defensive structure in their work, a structure which may be appropriate to the re-evoked infantile anxieties but is more than is required by external reality. Because of this defensive structure the conflicts which are projected into work cannot be resolved there and re-introjected in a more settled form. Thus the initial infantile anxieties remain at a high level.

One of the main forms of defence used in the group is denial. Quite involuntarily, the nurse does have a relationship with the suffering patient, and unconsciously shares this suffering, as well as experiencing a mixture of feelings such as guilt for not making the patient better and envy of the patient for being pampered. These intense and ambivalent feelings can be reduced by denying any relationship with the patient. This is achieved in various ways: the work is divided into a number of routine tasks so that the nurse performs patient-oriented tasks instead of nursing an actual patient; patients are referred to by symptom, or bed number, rather than by name; nurses move from ward to ward for no evident reason and with little warning; and so forth. The general aim is to make the work appear mechanical and deny its psychical reality.

Another form of defence used by the group involves splitting and projection. Nursing work carries a heavy responsibility; not only is this difficult to bear consistently, but also it conflicts with more irresponsible feelings, such as libidinal attachments to patients. This conflict can be reduced by splitting off from the self both responsible and irresponsible impulses, and projecting the former into more senior nurses and the latter into more junior (the five levels of nurse form a natural hierarchy for this). This process creates both responsible and irresponsible roles, and their incumbents, accepting the projections, act out these roles. Thus discipline exercised by the 'responsible' nurses becomes unnecessarily harsh, and deviant behaviour by the 'irresponsible' exaggeratedly so. A further effect of this is the practice of 'upward delegation'. Junior nurses feel dependent on their seniors, into whom they have projected all their responsible parts, while seniors feel that they cannot trust their juniors, into

INDIVIDUALS AND THE GROUP

whom they have projected all their irresponsible parts. The outcome is that all delegation is up rather than down.

A related form of defence is withdrawal. Making decisions which may affect the recovery, and even the life, of patients may arouse intense anxiety. This can be reduced by avoiding any individual decision, using various devices; an overly elaborate task list is provided, specifying in great detail the way in which tasks are to be performed (or, in other words, reliance is made on a Bible); all tasks are deemed to be equally important, whether quite routine or genuinely life-and-death matters; any decision which has to be taken by an individual is checked at a multiplicity of levels; and so forth. The general aim is to distance the individual nurse from any decision and possible guilt for its effects.

These defences have a seriously disruptive effect on the manifest task of the hospital. Denial prevents patients from feeling cherished as well as interfering with training; splitting and projection result in unnecessary concentration of effort on discipline and the loss of the potential benefits of (downward) delegation; and withdrawal means that decisions are taken only with great reluctance – and then without adequate preparation. Thus the general pattern is one of unnecessary rigidity in an institution which requires substantial flexibility.

Not only do these defences stand in the way of work, but they also mould the institution in such a way that it fails to support the individual nurse in mastering her own anxiety. The general way in which this failure is manifest is that group behaviour is based on avoiding anxieties rather than confronting them and testing them against reality. Thus there is little possibility of individual nurses' internal conflicts being worked through in the group and re-introjected in a relatively settled form; in other words, anxiety remains at a high level – one which is determined more by phantasy than by reality.

As well as failing to provide a framework for dealing with primary individual anxieties the group also generates significant secondary anxieties. The extensive rigidity of the system, with its task-lists and insistence that all jobs are of equal importance, means that, because of the natural variations in the needs of patients, work loads vary considerably over time, often suddenly and unpredictably. In times of overwork nurses experience anxieties related to work being inadequately done, while in times of underemployment feelings of guilt are aroused; the general air of uncertainty and imminent crisis serves only to reinforce anxiety. In addition, the sudden movement between wards arouses similar anxieties, and also the specifically depressive anxiety of not having prepared adequately to leave patients and colleagues and of not being able to mourn their loss subsequently. The splitting-off and projection of their responsible parts, and the general withdrawal from decision-making, makes nurses feel devalued, particularly as they occupy such ostensibly responsible roles in society at large. Thus the normal satisfaction expected from work – personal relations, creativity, and so forth – are removed, and indeed replaced by stress.

But perhaps the greatest problem of the institution is that its defects are inherently self-perpetuating. For the nurses who leave are, on the whole, the very ones who have the capacity to confront anxieties and are not content to evade them indefinitely. They are precisely those nurses who would have the emotional capacity to change the system.

In this case study the group functions badly because it has found no way to resolve projected conflicts. Finding a way to do this may be difficult, but one possibility is the creation of a subgroup specifically, if unconsciously, for this purpose. This is the route followed in the second case study.

This case is based on the work of Jaques and his associates on the functioning of an engineering factory.[11] The main group I am concerned with is a department of the factory consisting of some sixty workers and two managers, but I am also concerned with a subgroup consisting of the two managers and three of the workers, acting as workers' representatives. The manifest purpose of this subgroup, or committee, is to discuss and negotiate the details of working arrangements.

When dealing with routine matters the tone of the subgroup's discussion is constructive, with each side, that is workers' representatives and management, stressing that good relations both exist and are important. However, when more substantive

INDIVIDUALS AND THE GROUP

issues arise, for example the possibility of moving from payments based on piece-rates to a flat rate of pay, sharp disagreements occur – even when, as is the case in this example, each side individually favours the change. At such times workers feel that they cannot trust the management, while the managers, on the other hand, re-emphasize their faith in the workers. However, these feelings are only expressed to colleagues on the same side, not to the opposing side. Despite these conscious, but uncommunicated, feelings working relations on the shop floor continue to be good. But in the committee room the manifest purpose becomes dominated by unconscious attitudes, and little progress is made on any substantive issues.

In order to understand what is occurring at the unconscious level we must recognize that the committee is a subgroup of the main group, and take account of the attitudes of the rest of the department, that is, the floor workers, to the committee, and also of the committee to the floor workers.

The floor workers unconsciously split the managers into good managers, that is, those they work with, and bad, that is, the same managers in the committee. They project their hostile and destructive impulses into their representatives, seeing these as stooges, or pawns who will be outwitted by management. This is not so that the representatives themselves become bad, but so that they can deflect this hostility on to the bad committee managers. At the same time they project their good impulses directly into the good work managers. This splitting and projection allows good relations to be maintained at the conscious reality level, while at the same time reinforcing individual defences against both depressive and paranoid anxiety at the unconscious phantasy level. Projecting good impulses into the work managers allows floor workers to re-introject good relations and preserve these managers from harm, thus alleviating depressive anxiety. Projecting bad impulses into their representatives allows hostility to be deflected away from floor workers, and in fact into the committee managers, thus alleviating paranoid anxiety.

Workers' representatives are able to reduce the depressive anxiety of their own bad impulses destroying their good

69

relations with management by accepting the projections of the floor workers. Then in expressing any hostility towards managers they are simply acting as representatives of the floor workers – at the psychic as well as the reality level. This reduction of depressive anxiety is reinforced by the defence of retreating from depressive to paranoid mechanisms, as in displaying unnecessary hostility and suspicion, particularly at times when deep anxieties are aroused, that is, at times of impending change.

Managers counter this paranoid hostility shown by workers' representatives by idealizing workers, for example by emphasizing their trust in them. This has the effect of reducing the unconscious sense of guilt which arises from managers exercising day-to-day authority over workers, and also of placating the resulting hostility of workers (which in turn reduces managers' paranoid anxieties). These paranoid hostilities expressed by workers' representatives and idealizations by management are complementary, and indeed self-reinforcing: the greater the hostility the greater the need for idealization, and the greater the idealization the greater the depressive anxiety and thus the retreat into paranoid hostility.

In summary, this case shows how a subgroup may be used to contain some of the unconscious conflicts of the main group, and allow the main group to proceed with its manifest purpose relatively unhampered by unconscious phantasy relations. From the viewpoint of the group as a whole this process is reasonably successful: the department works well. But, nevertheless, the committee is singularly unsuccessful at its manifest task, at least when there is any serious work to be done. But this is not surprising, as the real purpose of the subgroup is something quite different.

Appendix[12]

In this technical appendix I show that whatever 'reasonable' mechanism a group may adopt in making its choices these choices will be inherently irrational.

INDIVIDUALS AND THE GROUP

Let A be the set of alternatives over which the group can choose. A preference ordering is a binary relation on A (that is a relation which compares any two distinct elements of A) which is complete, asymmetric and transitive. Thus if P is a preference ordering then for any distinct elements X, Y and Z of A either XPY or YPX but not both, and also if XPY and YPZ then XPZ (where XPY means that X is preferred to Y, and so forth).

I shall denote the group by G. Each member of G has a preference ordering; an array of such orderings, one for each member of G, is a profile. I am concerned with the connection between the profile and the choices the group makes, or, to be more precise, with specifying the relation which determines the group's preference ordering given *any* possible profile for the group.

To avoid trivial cases it is necessary to impose three requirements on this relation. The first requirement, unanimity, is that if everyone in the group prefers X to Y, say, then the group prefers X to Y: if all members of G rank X above Y, which profile I shall write as

$$G \quad X \quad Y$$

then XPY. The second requirement, relevance, is that in ordering X and Y the group takes account only of its various members' orderings of X and Y: if there are two profiles which agree, for everyone, on the ranking of X and Y, and XPY under the first profile, then XPY under the second. The third requirement, plurality, is that the group's ordering does not reflect the ordering of one particular member (a dictator) whatever the orderings of other members: there is no member of G such that for every profile and every pair of alternatives X and Y we have XPY whenever this member ranks X above Y. These three requirements would seem to be the absolute minimum required for the mechanism to be seen as being reasonable.

I will show that these three requirements, and transitivity, imply a contradiction, which is to say that if the requirements are fulfilled then the group's ordering may be intransitive.[13] Consider a subgroup, that is a non-empty subset of G, say E, and

INDIVIDUALS AND THE GROUP

its complement in G, say F. If, given the profile

$$\begin{array}{ccc} E & X & Y \\ F & Y & X \end{array}$$

we have XPY, then E is said to be decisive for X over Y.

If E is decisive for X over Y, then it is decisive over any other distinct pair of alternatives, say V and W. To see this consider the following profile

$$\begin{array}{ccccc} E & V & X & Y & W \\ F & Y & W & V & X \end{array}$$

Using the independence assumption in each case, unanimity implies that VPX, the decisiveness of E implies that XPY and unanimity implies that YPW. It follows from transitivity that VPW, which, in this case, is to say that E is decisive for V over W. This argument assumes that X, Y, V and W are all distinct, but may readily be modified to cover the cases where some of these elements are the same. Thus if E is decisive over any pair it is decisive over all pairs, in which case I shall simply refer to E as being decisive.

If E is decisive and everyone in E prefers X to Y, then XPY regardless of the preferences of those in F. To see this consider the profile

$$\begin{array}{cccc} E & X & Z & Y \\ F & & Z & \end{array}$$

(the specification for F indicating that members of F rank Z above both X and Y but may have any rankings of X and Y). The decisiveness of E implies that XPZ and unanimity implies that ZPY, so that, using transitivity, XPY as required.

It follows that a subgroup with only one member cannot be decisive, for otherwise that member would be a dictator, contravening plurality. Thus there are some non-decisive subgroups. Consider one such, say D, together with a second subgroup with only one member, say E, and the complement of the

INDIVIDUALS AND THE GROUP

union of D and E, say F. Then consider the following profile

D	X	Y	Z
E	Z	X	Y
F	Y	Z	X

We have YPZ because E is non-decisive and ZPX because D is non-decisive, so that, using transitivity, YPX, which is to say that the union of D and E is non-decisive.

Thus adding an individual to a non-decisive subgroup does not make the subgroup decisive. Repeating such additions eventually shows that G itself is non-decisive, which contradicts unanimity.

This contradiction implies that there is in general no way of obtaining a transitive ordering for the group from its profile if the three minimal requirements are to be adhered to, which is to say that any reasonable mechanism which a group will adopt in making its choices will be irrational.

For simplicity of exposition I have not allowed for the possibility of individuals, or the group, being indifferent between two alternatives rather than preferring either, but it is straightforward to incorporate this possibility.

Chapter 5

Groups and society

The understanding of individual behaviour developed in chapters 2 and 3 may be seen as one of the foundations of a psychoanalytical theory of society – what I have called the behavioural component of such a theory. And the understanding of group processes developed in chapter 4 may be seen as an extension to this, as the interface between the behavioural component and the aggregation component – the pillars of the theory. But we still need a keystone to complete the edifice: this is provided by the aggregation component which I develop in this chapter.

By such an aggregation component I mean a specification of how the underlying aims of the members of society are translated, through the various groups to which these members belong, into the institutions adopted by society. If the underlying aim of everyone in society was peace then we might reasonably expect these aims to be translated into a peaceful society. And if everyone were to want war we might reasonably expect to find a war-torn society. In most cases, and in all interesting ones, the outcome will be less obvious. If one large section of the community longs for peace and another large section longs for war, do we observe a peaceful or a war-torn community? Peace would distress one section of society and war would distress another. We cannot expect to find the hawks waging war on the doves, for a fight, to be satisfying, must have two active parties. We might

GROUPS AND SOCIETY

expect a somewhat polarized society: a warrior class of knights fighting one another, and occasionally the other class; and a parallel class of monks praying for one another, and also for the warriors. However, this is but speculation. To be more precise we need an aggregation theory.

This aggregation theory will have to specify, at one and the same time, what social institution emerges and what pattern of groups accompanies, or supports, this institution – that is to say, what groups are active and what are latent. As we shall justify later, the social outcome is, in effect, simply the wish of the dominant group or groups, so that the problem of specifying the social outcome may be seen as that of exploring what is meant by dominant in this context. If, in the above example, only the monks see themselves as belonging to a group, in a sense of identifying with other members of the group, then the dominant group will be that of the monks, and society will be predominantly peaceful, the peace shattered only by occasional outbursts by individual, and thus relatively powerless, warriors.

There is a large number of potential groups in society. Simple calculation tells us that if there are N members of society then there are two raised to the power of N, less one, possible groups – for example, over a million billion possible groups in a roomful of fifty people. Not all, and indeed only a small proportion, of these will be active at any one time, that is to say, will be acting, albeit unconsciously, in unison. The remainder will be latent.

Latent groups, although they do not exist in the sense of their members being tied together by identification, may still be important; the possibility of their becoming active may influence the behaviour, and even the existence, of active groups. Monks may well temper their demands for universal love if they fear that by provoking individual knights too far they will cause them to band together. Or members of individual trade unions may consider themselves to be just that rather than identified with any wider trade union movement, while managers may consider themselves as belonging to their individual firms rather than any employers' federation. In this case the group of all trade unionists is latent, as is that of all employers. But if one of these groups becomes active, for example if all managers start to feel that they have a common cause and act as an employers' federation, then the other group may also become active: unionists may combine in a wider trade union movement as a defence against the paranoid anxiety of being harmed by the employers. This possibility may be enough to keep the employers' federation group latent.

As there is a large number of possible groups, many of which may be important even though latent, it will not be easy to follow the aims of members of society, through the ever-shifting sands of the groups to which they may belong, to the social outcome. To cut through this tangled undergrowth I shall proceed axiomatically: I shall suggest what general properties we might reasonably expect a society's institutional arrangements to satisfy, and then explore the implications of these properties. The intuition underlying this approach is straightforward, although its formalization is a little complex; I shall therefore treat the problem quite informally for the time being, and only formalize it in the appendix to this chapter.

Since the institutional arrangements adopted by society will reflect the underlying aims of its members, what we must specify, to be more precise, is the relation between the underlying aims of the members of society on the one hand and the institutional arrangements adopted by society on the other. By the former, that is, the underlying aims of the members of the society, I mean their manifest aims as would, given the appropriate opportunities, be expressed in their choices – regardless of whether these are compatible with their conscious wishes or not. If someone consistently takes up with partners who treat him badly then we ascribe to him the aim of having such a partner, even though his vehemently alleged aim is to have a more (obviously) loving relationship. This interpretation is not to imply that just because someone has something this is what he really wants: people may, from time to time, although not consistently, make genuine mistakes; and they may have no, or only a very limited, choice. It is clear that under this interpretation of aims the question of external irrationality, that is, of consistent discrepancies between aims and choices, does not arise.

GROUPS AND SOCIETY

By the second element in the relation, that is, the institutional arrangements adopted by society, I mean, at least in an ideal sense, a complete description of the entire institutional framework of society: its markets, its political parties, its armies, its churches, and so forth. Thus the constellation of, say, a market economy, democracy, volunteer army and established church together specifies one institution. And the constellation of a market economy, democracy, conscript army and established church together specifies another, different, institution. The fact that the two constellations have some elements in common is purely coincidental. Thus when I compare one institution with another the two are to be taken as mutually exclusive.

Although institutions should ideally be interpreted in this exclusive sense, in practice it is often tempting to consider particular elements of the institutional structure in isolation, as if they were separable from other elements. For example, we may want to discuss, as Freud did, religious organizations independently of other elements of the institutional constellation; or we may want to discuss political organizations in relative isolation. The extent to which this is a useful procedure will depend on the context: to examine military organizations independently of religious ones in a holy war would be a nonsense, but in other contexts it might be a useful approximation. This question is closely related to the question of what is meant by society, which I discussed in chapter 1. If we interpret society in the ideal sense as comprising all of mankind, then we cannot easily explore its military elements in isolation; but if we are prepared to consider an army as a society then such a procedure becomes more acceptable.

The axiomatic approach which I adopt may be motivated by an important observation of Bion's, which is explored by Wisdom. Bion suggests that the aims of the group, or of society, are a pool in which the aim of its members are dissolved even when the aims of the group and of all its members differ.[1] This conjecture is formalized by Wisdom in a way which is worth quoting at length.[2]

It seems clear, then, that in Bion's mind there may very well be a situation in which the unconscious attitude of the group as a whole is not reflected in the unconscious attitude of any single person in the group. This may be very remarkable but must be entertained at least as a possibility. In particular it would mean that the group might be in a state of dependence although none of the individual members might be in that state. This conclusion, however tentative, is of great importance in raising the possibility of unconscious group-attitudes that are totally emergent and totally at variance with the unconscious attitudes of its members....

How might such a constellation be possible? Can we even illustrate the possibility plausibly? Well, it seems possible that not one of the three billion people on Earth wants to destroy the environment, yet society is doing that. It is possible that no one at all wanted to produce inflation (there may of course now be some who want it to continue), yet societies did it. It is possible that no one, not even Göring, wanted World War II, except Hitler; but that example is marred by the intention of one man, though even then perhaps the *outcome* of war required the acquiescence of societies. And presumably no one at all wants a nuclear war....

Suppose a character is made up of individual urges, u's, along with object-relational dispositions, d's, which we may often for convenience lump together as propensities, p's; and also of social or group identifications, g's, all presumed unconscious. (I assume here that these sets are not developmental growths from one to another, but are three unconscious components of a person's character; so that we do not have to postulate different numbers in each set but may take each set to contain the same number, n, of factors.) A typical character factor will then be udg (or pg). We may then say that individual psychotherapy deals exclusively with the set of p's. For group therapy let a group activity of Bion type deal exclusively with group factors, G's. We may suppose then that a member of the group belongs to the group in virtue of identifying with these (or rejection of them) i.e. in virtue of his g's. The difference between the g's and the G's is that the g's are *identifications* of an individual with a group while the G's are *characters* of the group. And we may make the reasonable hypothesis that a leader's interpretation of the G's, or social influences upon them, affect the g's. In short we presume that development of a person's g's depends on social happenings. What, then are our questions? The fundamental one raised earlier concerned the possibility of changes among the g's modifying the d's. Here our question is, can there be states of the G's (and therefore of the g's) that have no counterpart at all among the d's?

I think the answer to such a question is not a 'yes' or a 'no' accompanied by some evidence, but a *theory of mental structure* that allows of (or does not) this hypothesis. It is conceivable that the g's need have no counterpart, though they usually would have, among the d's (while the d's would always have counterparts among the u's); possibly for some people there would not necessarily be counterparts among the u's; possibly for some people there would not necessarily be counterparts to the g's while for others there would always be – even close – counterparts.

Wisdom's examples of the Bion paradox of society reflecting the aims of none of its members are not particularly convincing (as indeed Wisdom suggests). If I am a coal miner I may not be so averse to a little environmental pollution. If I have a large mortgage and an index-linked salary I may be quite pleased with inflation. The war examples, as Wisdom notes, confuse outcomes with intentions; even faced with nuclear war some people may rather be dead than red, particularly if they believe that the reds will also be dead. None the less, the essence of Wisdom's observation is that it is important to have an explicit theoretical structure which allows, or rules out as the case may be, the possibility of the aims of society not reflecting the aims of any one of its members. In other words, we require some axioms whose properties, including the possibility or otherwise of the Bion paradox, we may then explore.

Before leaving the Bion paradox we should note that the question is whether the choices of society reflect the underlying, not just the conscious, aims of any of its members. If we only consider the conscious aims of the members we may well find these ignored in society's choices. Thus Wisdom's examples should also be questioned because they appear to concern predominantly conscious aims. To stay with the example of war, we may note Freud's exchange with Einstein on the subject.[3] Einstein (as does Wisdom) sees the prevalence of war over the ages as puzzling: war inflicts objective suffering on all involved, yet all efforts to banish war end in dismal failure. But in this case the puzzle is resolved by noting that the desire for peace expresses only the conscious wish. As we have seen, despite its objective physical horrors war may relieve internal anxiety, and satisfy the death instinct, sufficiently that, at the unconscious level, it becomes preferred to peace. As Freud noted in his reply to Einstein, it is fruitless to try to abolish man's aggressive impulses.

The basic axiom underlying the aggregation theory has its origins, albeit implicitly, in Edgeworth's *Mathematical Psychics*,[4] written in 1881, though it was made explicit only a little later, by Pareto.[5] Consider two possible institutional arrangements, say X and Y. For example, X may comprise a market economy, democracy, volunteer army, established church, and so forth – a complete description. The institution Y is a constellation which differs from this in some respect, and possibly in all respects. The aims of members of society take the form of preferences between X and Y; an individual either prefers X to Y or he prefers Y to X (or, in the limiting case, he is indifferent between the two). As I have noted, these aims, or preferences, are not necessarily conscious: they are simply the preferences, which are embodied in, or revealed by, the individual choices. For example, a liberal who has suffered conscription in his youth may be conscious only of preferring a volunteer army to a conscript one, or indeed preferring to have no army at all; but because of an unconscious envy of those now fortunate enough to escape his fate his actions may subtly but consistently support conscription.

If everyone in society prefers, in this sense, X to Y (or if at least one person prefers X and everyone else is indifferent), then I shall say that X dominates Y. An institution is *tenable* if it is not dominated by any other possible institution. The basic axiom, then, is that society adopts only tenable institutions. The motivation underlying this axiom is that if everyone prefers (in the underlying sense) some alternative to a given institution then we should not expect the given institution to prevail.

Consider, for example, a society in which all individuals' emotions are dominated by a mixture of envy of others who might possess something good, together with guilt for having anything good which others might lack. We should not expect to find any noticeable inequalities in this society, since the institutional arrangement of equality would dominate any other, unequal, institutional arrangement: both the envious poor and the guilty rich would prefer, albeit unconsciously in the case of the latter, a move towards equality. On the other hand, in a society where some individuals' emotions are dominated by greed and others' by masochistic self-denial we should expect to find significant inequalities. The institutional arrangement of equality would be dominated by an arrangement in which the greedy are rich and the self-denying are poor.

This basic axiom, however reasonable, is only a premise, and by its nature cannot be proven. But it is not a tautology, that is to say, it does not simply equate wishes with outcomes by definition. There may be genuine errors in achieving what is desired; the nuclear button may be pressed through a real misunderstanding. There may be problems of communication, particularly if society is to be interpreted in the strict sense as comprising the whole of mankind, although communication in this context need not be conscious but may simply be through unconscious identification. None the less, in the long run we might reasonably expect repeated mistakes to be corrected and consistent communications problems to be overcome. The concept of a tenable institution is thus to be seen as an ideal. Even if actual institutions are not always tenable, untenable institutions will not last long and will tend to be replaced by other institutions which, if not tenable themselves, become progressively closer to some tenable institution.

I have noted that problems of external rationality do not arise in this context. Provided that all individuals display internal rationality, no problems of internal rationality for society as a whole will arise either. If all individuals are rational in the internal sense and everyone prefers X to Y, and also everyone prefers Y to Z, then everyone will prefer X to Z. Thus the problem of internal rationality does not arise simply because we are only concerned with comparisons about which everyone agrees: the problem of making consistent group choices is trivial when the group is unanimous. But despite this internal and external rationality individuals in society will still resort to psychotic mechanisms which produce volatile behaviour, and this volatility will be manifest in the behaviour, or choices, of society itself.

It is important to ask whether, or rather in what cases, we can be sure that there exists some tenable institution; if tenable institutions never existed the axiom would be vacuous. Provided that individuals are rational in the internal sense, and provided that there are only a finite number of possible institutions available to society, then there will always be some tenable institution. If there were not then we would either have to have an ordering such as X dominates Y, Y dominates Z and Z dominates X; or alternatively we would have to have an ordering such as Y dominates Z, X dominates Y, W dominates X, and so forth indefinitely. In the first case society would be displaying internal irrationality, which, as we have seen, would mean that individuals were irrational in the internal sense. And in the second case we would need an infinite number of institutions.

As I have argued, the proviso that individuals be internally rational is quite unobjectionable. On the other hand, the proviso that the number of possible institutions be finite may seem more problematical: it would not be unreasonable to suppose that there is a continuum of, and thus infinitely many, possible institutions. However, this condition is only a sufficient rather than a necessary condition: there may well be a tenable institution even if the number of possible institutions is not finite, as the example below shows.

Although there will always be some tenable institution there may well be more than one; indeed, it may even be that all possible institutions are tenable. For example, if two expansionist superpowers are to divide the world then any of the infinitely many possible institutions, in this case any of the possible divisions of the world between them, is tenable. This is because, starting with any arbitrary division, any change, that is, any alternative division, must give one power more and the other less. The power which receives less will object to the change, so that the new division cannot dominate the original division. This implies that the original division, whatever it is, is tenable. This possibility of there being many tenable institutions is a problem: in the extreme case where all possible institutions are tenable the axiom is of as little help as it would be were there to be no tenable institution. I shall return to this problem later.

It is clear that the basic axiom resolves the question raised by

GROUPS AND SOCIETY

Bion, that is, whether it is possible that the aims of a society reflect the aims of none of its members: the axiom does *not* admit this possibility. Assume that when faced with two possible institutions, say X and Y, society adopts the institution X while no individual in society prefers X, so that the aim of society reflects the aim of none of its members. If we ignore the trivial case where all individuals are indifferent between X and Y (that is where they have no aims for society to reflect), then someone prefers Y to X, so that Y dominates X and society adopts Y rather than X – contrary to our assumption.

The aims of society may well reflect the aims of the various individuals in society without the institution adopted by society being the best possible institution according to the preference of any of its members. This is simply the natural process of compromise. Consider three possible institutions: a liberal regime (say X), a socialist regime (Y), and civil war (Z). Staunch liberals rank these in order X, Z, Y and staunch socialists in the order Y, Z, X. All institutions are tenable, and society may well adopt the compromise of civil war (Z) even though this is no one's most preferred institution.

There are two major inadequacies of the basic axiom. The first is that the premise, at least if interpreted as referring to an ideal, is quite unobjectionable: but as a consequence of this it is also quite weak. By this I mean that although the axiom does not rule out any institutions which we might reasonably expect society to adopt it does admit a large number of institutions which seem relatively unlikely to prevail. In other words, it is too generous in an undiscriminating way. This is the result of the axiom saying something in the case of unanimity but otherwise remaining silent. The second defect of the axiom is that it involves only the aims of the individuals in society, and not the opportunities which are open to them, either as individuals or, more importantly, as members of groups. This is clearly naive: some groups may be able to impose certain institutions on society which others cannot. If one, and only one, of the two superpowers dividing the world has nuclear arms this may well rule out all but one of the possible tenable divisions.

*

GROUPS AND SOCIETY

In the light of these defects I propose a second axiom, as a strengthening of, rather than an alternative to, the first. By taking account of the opportunities open to groups this axiom rules out some of the tenable institutions which society would appear unlikely to adopt. This second axiom also has its implicit origins in Edgeworth's *Mathematical Psychics*; it involves a concept, that of a stable institution, which is an extension of that of the core in game theory.

Consider a group of individuals in society, a group which may consist of only one individual at one extreme or of the whole of society at the other, though which more typically will be a proper group, that is, will consist of more than one but not all of the members of society. The group may be able to impose some particular institutions on society, but this is unlikely as large societies tend to be decentralized in some way, for example leaving religion to the church, politics to the state, and so forth. It is more likely that the group will be able to impose some set of institutions on society without being able to impose any particular institution in this set. Consider the following four possible institutions: high church and left government, say W; high church and right government (X); low church and left government (Y); and low church and right government (Z). The church, as a group, is able to impose a high church on society but has little influence on government. In this case the group could impose the set comprising the institutions W and X without being able either to impose W or to impose X. The set comprising the institutions W and X, which I shall write as (W,X), is thus one of the sets which the group can impose. But the church could also impose a low church on society, that is to say, impose the set (Y,Z). In general, then, there will be a whole family of sets of institutions which a group can impose on society: the family comprises a number of sets, each of which specifies a menu which the group can impose on society without being able to impose any particular dish listed on the menu.

If the group is small it may have very little influence; in this case its family will contain only a few sets, each of which is large. On the other hand, a large group may be able to exert a substantial influence, in which case its family will contain many

GROUPS AND SOCIETY

sets, some of which will be quite small. Power consists of having a family in which there is a large number of sets, that is, in having influence in many quarters, and also in which some of the sets are small, that is, in being able to exert his influence quite precisely. If one group is a subgroup of another then the latter (the large group) will have more influence than the former (the subgroup). Specifically, if the subgroup can impose some set then the large group can either impose this or it can impose a subset: if the small group can impose (X,Y) then the large group can either impose (X,Y) or impose X or impose Y. At the extreme, when the group comprises the whole of society, it can 'impose' any specific possible institution, since in this context a possible institution is simply an institution which society as a whole can achieve.

Now consider a possible institution, which I shall call X. Consider also a group, with its associated family of sets of institutions which it can impose on society. If there is some set in the family associated with the group such that everyone in the group prefers all institutions in this set to X (or, at least, given any such institution, one person prefers it and everyone else is indifferent), then I shall say that X is dominated in the group. An institution is *stable* if it is not dominated in any possible group – from single individuals to the whole of society. The second axiom, then, is that society adopts only stable institutions. The motivation underlying this axiom is that if some group both prefers and can impose some alternative (or set of alternatives) to a given institution, then we should not expect the given institution to prevail.

As with the first axiom, this second axiom, however reasonable, cannot be proven: it too is to be seen as an ideal. There will still be problems of communication and so forth, and indeed these will be more serious here. In the context of the first axiom communication involves identification within only one, admittedly large, group – society itself. But in the present context it involves some experimentation with a variety of groups, as well as identification within in each of these. The implication of this is that while the first axiom is, if anything, too weak, this second axiom may be too strong: any stable institution is certainly a

GROUPS AND SOCIETY

candidate for adoption by society, but certain other, non-stable, institutions may also be candidates.

As with tenable institutions, problems of internal or external rationality do not arise. But the problem of volatility remains, and now plays a more central role, since groups play a much larger part in the working of this second axiom than the purely nominal part, in the role of society itself, which they played in that of the first. Psychotic anxieties provoked, or awakened, by group membership now run rampant.

The second axiom is a strengthening of the first in that any stable institution is tenable but some tenable institutions may not be stable. To see that any stable institution is tenable recall that if an institution X is stable then it is not dominated in any group whatsoever, and in particular it is not dominated in society itself. Now society itself can impose any possible institution. This means that if X is not dominated in society then there is no alternative institution which everyone prefers, which is to say that X is a tenable institution. Intuitively it is clear that the converse of this is false, that is, there may be some institutions which are tenable but not stable: stable institutions have to satisfy the requirements of society itself, as do tenable ones, and, in addition, the requirements of all other groups. An example which I explore later justifies this intuition.

As with tenable institutions, it is possible, though less likely, for there to be many stable institutions. Let us return to the example of two superpowers dividing the world, but now with both of them armed and with the understanding that failure to reach agreement results in nuclear war and mutual destruction. The powers acting together can achieve any division, that is, institution, and no division dominates any other since one power would always gain and the other lose in any change. The only institution which either power alone can impose is mutual destruction, which is seen as being worse than any agreed division. Thus a given division cannot be dominated in any of the three possible groups (society itself and each power alone), which is to say that all divisions, or all institutions except mutual destruction, are stable. Mutual destruction, however, is not stable, and not even tenable.

GROUPS AND SOCIETY

I have shown that there will always be some tenable institution, at least provided that internal rationality prevails and there are only finitely many possible institutions. It is important to note that the corresponding property does *not* apply to stable institutions: there may well be no stable institution at all. Essentially, this is because an institution X may be dominated in one group, in that this group both prefers and can impose an alternative institution Y, while the institution Y is dominated in a second group, which both prefers and can impose the institution X; provided that the two groups have completely different memberships there is nothing inconsistent in this. This possibility is demonstrated more concretely in an example I explore below.

The fact that there may be no stable institution does not of itself detract from the usefulness of the second axiom. On the contrary, it identifies a fundamental source of instability in social arrangements – of swings between egalitarian revolutions and elitist counter-revolutions, between permissiveness and authoritarianism, and so forth.

If there are no stable institutions then any existing institution, and of course there must be some existing institution since an institution is simply a description of the arrangements of society, will be short-lived; it will soon be dominated in some group and thus replaced by an alternative institution, which will also be short-lived. This fundamental cause of instability is independent of the volatility of individuals in groups: both may co-exist, and reinforce each other.

The specification of the tenable institutions in society depends on two parameters: the institutions which are possible and the preferences of the various members of society. The specification of the stable institutions depends, in addition to these two parameters, on the various institutions or sets of institutions which each possible group in society can impose on the whole of society. (Also relevant, though I have not discussed this in detail, is the way in which individual preferences change in, or are moulded by, the group.) This interpretation allows us to express the distinction between the behavioural and aggregation components of the theory more precisely: the behavioural component explains these parameters, that is, explains individuals' aims, the power of groups and so forth; and the aggregation component builds on these parameters to show how they determine the nature and institutions of society.

I shall illustrate the workings of the two axioms with a simple example. There are three religious denominations, Christians, Jews and Moslems; for simplicity I shall assume that each denomination is indivisible, that is, treat each as if it were an individual. We are concerned with the extent to which these denominations form alliances with one another, that is, whether they exist as isolated denominations, as a pair with one excluded denomination, or in a grand coalition as a triad. This means that there are five possible institutions: isolation, which I shall call Z; the triad (Y); the pairing of Jews and Moslems but excluding Christians (XC); that of Christians and Moslems, excluding Jews (XJ); and finally that of Christians and Jews, excluding Moslems (XM).

There are seven possible groups in society: Christians, Jews and Moslems together, that is, society as a whole, which I shall call CJM; Jews and Moslems (JM); Christians and Moslems (CM); Christians and Jews (CJ); Christians alone (C); Jews alone (J); and Moslems alone (M). Society as a whole can impose any institution. Jews and Moslems together can agree to combine, that is, to impose the institution XC, or they can agree to remain as individuals, that is, to impose the institution Z. In the same way the group CM can impose XJ and Z, and the group CJ can impose XM and Z. Christians alone can only rule out the triad or any pairing involving Christians, which is to say that they can impose the set (XC, Z): they can ensure that either XC or Z is adopted but cannot determine which. In the same way the groups J and M can impose the sets (XJ, Z) and (XM, Z) respectively. The various groups and the institutions or sets of institutions which they can impose are summarized as follows.

Group	Institutions
CJM	XC, XJ, XM, Y, Z
JM	XC, Z

GROUPS AND SOCIETY

CM	XJ, Z
CJ	XM, Z
C	(XC, Z)
J	(XJ, Z)
M	(XM, Z)

Each denomination prefers to be in a pairing, but does not mind with whom; if it achieves this it is in a majority, so is relatively protected, and at the same time has a minority to project its death instinct into and then persecute. Failing this, each denomination would prefer the triad, since at least it is safe from the attacks of others. After this, each denomination prefers isolation, since then it can only be persecuted by an equal, and not by a larger pair. The worst institution is a pairing which excludes the denomination. These preferences are summarized as follows.

Denominations	*Ranking*
Christians	XJ/XM, Y, Z, XC
Jews	XC/XM, Y, Z, XJ
Moslems	XC/XJ, Y, Z, XM

A institution is tenable if it is not dominated by any other institution, that is, if there is no institution which everyone prefers (or at least someone prefers and everyone else is indifferent to). The institution Z is not tenable, since each denomination prefers Y. But there is no institution which everyone prefers to Y: Christians would object to XC (in that they prefer Y to XC), Jews would object to XJ, Moslems would object to XM and all denominations would object to Z. Thus the institution Y is tenable. Also, there is no institution which everyone prefers to XC: Jews (for example) would object to Y, Z and XJ, while Moslems would object to XM. Thus the institution XC is also tenable. Analogous arguments show that the institutions XM and XJ are tenable. Thus the tenable institutions are the triad and all three possible pairings.

An institution is stable if it is not dominated in any possible group. The institution Z is not stable as it is not tenable, that is, it

GROUPS AND SOCIETY

is dominated in the group CJM. The institution Y is dominated in the group JM: this group can impose XC, and both its members prefer XC to Y. The institution XC, in turn, is dominated in the group CM: this group can impose XJ, one of its members (Christians) prefers XJ to XC, and the other member (Moslems) is indifferent between the two. Analogous arguments show that the institutions XJ and XM are also dominated, in the groups CJ and CM respectively. Thus all institutions are dominated in some group and there are no stable institutions.

In this example we should, then, expect to observe a continually changing pattern of alliances. Given the high priority attached by all denominations to being in some pairing we might expect this changing pattern to consist of some pairing forming, only to break up when one of the pair is approached by the excluded denomination, leading to a new pairing, break-up, and so forth.

I shall now alter the example by changing the denominations' preferences but leaving the remaining structure unchanged. In this new example each denomination is concerned only with the size of the coalition it is in: the larger the better. These new preferences may be summarized as follows (where, as before, XJ/XM denotes indifference between XJ and XM, and so forth).

Denomination	Ranking		
Christians	Y,	XJ/XM,	XC/Z
Jews	Y,	XC/XM,	XJ/Z
Moslems	Y,	XC/XJ,	XM/Z

Arguments similar to those employed in the original example show that the institution Y remains tenable, but that this is now the only tenable institution. Further, the institution Y is now stable, and indeed the only stable institution. In this revised example we may, then, more concretely, expect the triad to prevail.

A more general, but still simple, example of the workings of the axioms concerns the satisfaction of the material wants of society.[6] There are a number of commodities, such as food, clothing, housing, and so forth. Each individual is endowed with

GROUPS AND SOCIETY

various amounts of these commodities: the farmer may have food, the craftsman clothing, the landlord housing, and so forth. Strictly speaking, the possible institutions in society are all the various allocations of these commodities to the individuals. However, it is more useful to interpret the various mechanisms which produce these allocations as the institutions: mechanisms such as the market, where people can buy and sell what they will without restriction; price controls, where necessities, say, can only be bought and sold at some fixed prices; rationing, where necessities can only be bought and sold in limited quantities; and so forth. Individuals' preferences between the institutions depend only on the bundles of commodities they receive under them: for example, a heavy eater may do well under a system of price controls and thus rank it high (assuming food to be classified as a necessity), while a heavy drinker may do badly and rank it low (assuming drink to be classified as a luxury).

The sets of institutions which a group can impose on society depend on the endowments of the members of the group. The group can, if it sees fit, refrain from trading with outsiders so that members only exchange commodities with one another. Assume that the group agrees to some particular redistribution of its own endowments; it can then impose this on society, although it cannot ordain what redistributions may occur in the rest of society. The set of institutions in which the group has this particular redistribution and the rest of society has any possible redistribution of its endowments is thus one set which the group can impose. If the group agrees to some second redistribution of its endowments this defines a second set which the group can impose. By considering all possible redistributions within the group we arrive at the family of all sets of institutions which the group can impose.

The parameters of the problem are now defined: we have specified the possible institutions, the preferences of the individuals, and the sets of institutions which the groups can impose on society. It remains to investigate which institutions, if any, are stable.

Consider the institution of the market, by which I mean, to be more precise, the social arrangement in which people buy and sell commodities as they see fit at some common prices, these prices being such that the total desired purchases of each commodity are the same as the total desired sales. Assume that some group prefers some allocation Y to the allocation X associated with the institution of the market. This means that all members of the group prefer the bundle of goods which they receive under Y to that which they receive under X (ignoring, for simplicity, the possibility of some members being indifferent). Now the bundle which a member receives under X is, in terms of his preferences, the best bundle he can afford, that is, the best bundle of all those whose cost, at the given market prices, does not exceed the value of his endowment. It follows that if he prefers the bundle he receives under Y then this bundle must cost more than the value of his endowment. Since this applies to all members of the group the total cost of the group's allocation under Y must be more than the total value of the group's endowment. But this means that the group is unable to impose the institution producing the allocation Y: its endowment is insufficient. What I have shown, then, is that, given any arbitrary group, there is no allocation which the group both prefers to the market allocation and can achieve. In other words, the institution of the market is stable: this is the case whatever the preferences and whatever the endowments of the individuals.

In small societies there may also be some other stable institutions, but it is a remarkable fact that if the society is sufficiently large and diverse then there is precisely one stable institution: that of the market.[7] This example explains why the institution of the market is so prevalent in society, and why the more successful alternatives (such as decentralized, as opposed to centralized, planning) are those which produce allocations not too different from those produced by the market.

I shall illustrate the theory developed here with two case studies. The first concerns the workings of a modern university in the south of England. The society I shall be concerned with, although of course this is not a closed society in the ideal sense, is that of the teaching staff of the university. The staff numbers about 350, the large majority being in arts and social science.

GROUPS AND SOCIETY

Staff are loosely grouped by subject area but with no formal departmental structure: no department budgets or territories. Because it is a young university the age distribution of the staff is unusual: a disproportionately large number are in their middle years, with only relatively few either young or old.

The duties of the teaching staff are threefold: to teach undergraduate and postgraduate students; to engage in original enquiry and research; and to administer the university as a whole. The amount of time devoted to teaching is determined fairly mechanically by the number of students, and can be varied only marginally by the individual teacher. This time, including preparation and so forth, is of the order of a quarter of the working year. The remaining three-quarters are to be devoted to research and administration (and, unofficially, to outside work and leisure).

Original research is difficult: not in that it requires any particular intellectual gifts, but in that it requires some ill-defined sense of creativity – creativity is involved in posing questions, intellectual ability in answering them. Intellectual skills may be acquired consciously, and thus relatively straightforwardly, but creativity is only acquired unconsciously, through learning from experience in the sense used in chapter 2. Original research, then, is difficult to instigate; also, by its nature, it must be instigated alone, or possibly in a very small team, rather than in any proper group. On the other hand, it is straightforward for the individual to become involved in administration: the problems are given to him, and as administration is essentially a group activity the individual can lose his responsibility in the group.

Given this general background we may specify the parameters of the society: the institutions available to it, the preferences of its members, and the institutions which the various groups in society can impose.

The possible institutions are the various ways of living and working together in an academic community. Two aspects of this are of particular interest. The first is whether the university is primarily research-oriented or administration-oriented. A research-oriented community is one in which individuals devote most of their (non-teaching) time to original research, within a loose and minimal administrative framework. In an administration-oriented community individuals devote most of their time to ensuring that research, teaching and so forth are 'run properly', but little time to research itself – much effort is spent drilling the troops but little fighting the enemy. The second aspect is whether the university is primarily an open or a closed community. An open community is one in which individuals are encouraged to work with and learn from people in other communities: in government, business and so forth. In a closed community the outside world is more split-off, to be dealt with only indirectly, through the university itself, if indeed at all. We have then, in simplified terms, four possible institutions: a research-oriented open community, which I shall call RO; a research-oriented closed one (RC); an administration-oriented open community (AO); and an administration-oriented closed one (AC).

The conscious aims of the members of the university are relatively straightforward: everyone prefers a research-oriented community to an administration-oriented one, and an open community to a closed one. But the underlying aims are a little different. For our purposes the members of the community may be divided into two classes. One class consists of those who feel that they can be creative; to keep the terminology simple I shall refer to these as bees. The other class consists of those who do not feel that they can be creative, whom I shall refer to, again for simplicity only, as ants. It is to be emphasized that this division is essentially internal and subjective rather than external and objective. A bee is simply someone who feels, albeit unconsciously, that he can do creative work, regardless of how much he produces or of how this is received by his peers. And an ant is someone who feels that he cannot be creative, even if what he does produce is of real value.

The ant (as indeed the bee) derives a significant part of his livelihood from the university; he thus feels that he must give something in return. Feeling that he cannot give creative work, the production of which is the overt purpose of the university, the ant experiences a sense of unconscious guilt. And alongside

GROUPS AND SOCIETY

this he also experiences unconscious envy as he sees his colleague, the bee, being creative: as Melanie Klein notes, others' creativity is the ultimate object of envy.[8] These two emotions, of guilt and envy, may be defended against efficiently in an administration-oriented community. By becoming involved in administration the ant can feel that he is doing something useful for the university (or at least more useful than outside work or leisure), thus diminishing his sense of guilt. But his involvement in administration also hinders the bee's research, thus diminishing his, the ant's sense of envy: firstly, the bee is forced to join in the activity – become a member of the ant's committee, answer his memoranda, and so forth; and secondly, the aim of administration is to ensure that people do things other than those which they would do in the absence of administration – which in the bee's case is research. In short, the ant unconsciously prefers an administration-oriented community to a research-oriented one.

As is the case with all defences, the defence, against unconscious guilt and envy, of engaging in administration is not completely successful: there remains some unconscious sense that this is a sham. Exposure to people in different communities, such as government or business, tends to expose this sham. But perhaps more importantly, the feelings of hostility embodied in the ant's envy of the bee (envy being an externalization of the death instinct) cannot comfortably be projected into the bee, for the bee is both the good part of the ant (what he would want to be) and his good breast (the overt purpose for the university's existence and thus of the ant's nourishment). Projecting this hostility into the bee would arouse depressive anxieties in the ant. His hostility is thus displaced on to outsiders, who accordingly become split-off. Thus the ant unconsciously prefers a closed community, which allows such splitting, to an open one.

The bee's feelings about research and administration are relatively straightforward: he prefers a research-oriented community to an administration-oriented one. But his feelings about open and closed communities are more complex. The bee unconsciously experiences some resentment against the ant for attempting to destroy his work and creativity, which he experiences in a paranoid way as attempts to destroy him. But he too cannot express his hostility too directly: firstly, he fears the ant's retaliation; and secondly, he fears that inter-sibling quarrelling will tear his family apart, and destroy the university which provides him with the opportunity to be creative. Thus the bee also displaces his hostility on to outsiders, who become split-off. The bee also then unconsciously prefers a closed community to an open one.

The discussion so far specifies each class's preferences as between research and administration on the one hand and between an open and a closed community on the other, but it does not specify the ant's ranking of the institutions RC and AO nor the bee's ranking of the institutions RO and AC. Since, for both ants and bees, feelings about open and closed communities arise mainly from those about research and administration, I shall assume that preferences between research and administration dominate those between open and closed communities. This implies that ants prefer the institution AO to RC and that bees prefer RO to AC. The underlying preferences of both classes may then be summarized as follows.

Class	Ranking
Ants	AC, AO, RC, RO
Bees	RC, RO, AC, AO

There are many possible groups within the university. The apparently obvious grouping into subject areas is in fact weak, mainly because these areas have no formal identity as departments. The dominant division, at least at the unconscious level, is between ants and bees. This crystallization generates three possible groups: the university as a whole; ants alone; and bees alone.

The university as a whole can impose any of the four possible institutions. As regards the two other groups, there is a fundamental asymmetry between research and administration. Research is essentially individualistic, even if carried out in a team: the individual researcher, or team, carries out his own

GROUPS AND SOCIETY

work and is not concerned with what the rest of the university does. But administration is essentially collective: by its nature it involves administering others, not just oneself. This asymmetry implies that any (reasonably large) group can, if it wants, impose an administration-oriented community on the university but that no proper group can impose a research-oriented community. In the same way, any group can impose an open community — if one door is open then the house is open; but no proper group can impose a closed community. The various institutions which the groups in the university can impose are thus as follows.

Group	Institutions
University	RO, RC, AO, AC
Ants	AO
Bees	AO

I have now specified the relevant parameters, and can consider which institutions are tenable and which, if any, are stable. It is clear that everyone prefers the institution RC to RO so that RO is dominated, and that everyone prefers AC to AO so that AO is dominated. However, there is no institution which everyone prefers to RC and no institution which everyone prefers to AC, so that neither RC nor AC is dominated. Thus the tenable institutions are RC and AC. This means that only RC and AC can conceivably be stable. However, ants prefer the institution AO to RC, and can also impose AO; thus RC cannot be stable. But there is no institution which either ants or bees both prefer to AC and can impose, so that AC is stable. Thus there is precisely one stable institution: the administration-oriented closed community. This is despite the facts that everyone consciously prefers research to administration and an open to a closed community, and that even unconsciously the greater part of the university may prefer research to administration.

This predicted state of affairs accords well with reality. In fact, the university has a markedly administrative-oriented ethos which has a pervasive effect on both those who explicitly engage in administration and those who do not. Relative to some comparable universities *over twice* as much time is devoted by staff as a whole to administration, and even more by junior staff. Even senior members of staff can do very little without detailed administrative approval – less than can their junior colleagues in other universities. Although the university professes to be open in fact it ensures that there is little real personal contact between its members and outsiders; it does this by requiring that most contact be through the university itself rather than between individuals. Thus the sorts of arrangements which are easily achieved in other universities, arrangements such as consultancies, external research finance, and so forth are only achieved with difficulty, if at all.

A couple of examples illustrate this state of affairs quite efficiently. The first occurred at a meeting of faculty board, a large body representing nearly half of the teaching staff, at which a request was made for permission for two foreign scholars to visit the university for a few days to work privately with a small team in the university on the roots of racial conflict. The two in question were South Africans, and their proposed visit had the specific endorsement of a prominent black South African leader – in fact a bishop and Nobel peace prize winner who had only some months earlier received an honorary degree from the university itself. By a large majority the board refused the request – thus efficiently discouraging both creative research and links with outsiders. In the second example an offer of research funding was received from a major charity, one of the main research sponsors in the country. If accepted, this would have paid for some replacement teaching, and indeed have left the university with a significant financial surplus. But the offer was rejected unanimously by those voting on it – again discouraging both research and outside links.

The university then does not function well in that it does not generate the open, enquiring ethos which its members would enjoy. This is particularly wasteful because the university has a large number of potentially creative people and a structure, of no departments, which superficially would seem ideal for creativity.

Although it is not strictly relevant in the present context, it is of some interest to enquire why this university differs from other universities, many of which are both research-oriented and open. As I have noted, the problem is *not* that there are too many ants and too few bees, but rather than the ants hold sway over the bees. There would seem to be three factors which are relevant to this. Firstly, the organization of subject areas into loose groupings with no formal departmental structure encourages the crystallization of groups along lines, such as ants and bees, other than departmental ones. If there were a formal departmental framework individuals' inner conflicts could be played out in inter-departmental rivalries, with no pro-administration or pro-research implications. Secondly, being in a rural area, the university is the centre of the social and emotional, as well as the working, lives of many members of the staff. Having relatively little contact with people in other professions staff are more likely to be wary of such people, and thus keep them at a distance. The third factor is the unusual age structure. One aspect of this is that many members of the university have little experience of working in other universities, which exacerbates their fear of outsiders. Perhaps more importantly, in a more mature university with a more representative age structure there will still be some younger ants, but a disproportionate number of ants will be near to retirement, having done the bulk of their creative work while younger. On account of this earlier work they will feel neither guilty nor envious of their bee colleagues. Indeed, they may encourage such colleagues, in a more reparative and integrative way, so that the influence of ants as a whole is reduced.

The second 'case' I consider is based in the two central, and related, aspects of Freud's view of society which I discussed in chapter 1: that emphasizing the primal horde, and that emphasizing the renunciation of instinctual pleasure. I do not aim to offer a general assessment of these rich themes, but simply to examine their relation to the theory developed here.

The theme of the final essay of *Totem and Taboo*,[9] it may be recalled is that the original form of society was that of Darwin's primal horde, with a powerful male keeping the other males under his absolute control and the females for his own gratification; this state of affairs persisted until the subjugated males

GROUPS AND SOCIETY

killed and devoured the leader, and possessed the females. The unconscious memory of this primal crime, in the form of guilt and defences against its re-occurrence, explains a wide range of social phenomena, particularly the incest taboo. As is apparent, this theme both involves the concept of a collective mind and is essentially diachronic. It has, then, little common ground with the theory developed here, which is essentially individualistic and synchronic. But there is one observation that the theory can offer, and this is that the supposed original institution of the primal horde was unlikely to have been a stable institution.

The group consisting of the subjugated males, not to mention the females, would presumably prefer an institution in which all males and females could pair with one another; this group might also be expected to have the power to impose such an institution, through the force of its numbers. This observation, that the institution of the primal horde is unlikely to have been stable, may be taken as supporting Freud's hypothesis of the primal crime of the murder of the leader. Alternatively, and perhaps more persuasively, it may be taken as implying that the institution of the primal horde was too precarious to have existed, at least for sufficient time to be of any interest. Unstable institutions do not last long.

One of Freud's basic themes in *The Future of an Illusion*[10] is that the entire edifice of civilization is based on the renunciation of instinctual pleasure, since civilization is built by work rather than by erotic gratification. This renunciation of pleasure is achieved only through coercion, so we experience one part of society, indeed the smaller part, coercing the other, larger, part. This results not only in a loss of gratification by the majority, but also in a similar loss by the minority. This theme does not depend on the concept of a collective mind nor is it essentially diachronic. There is therefore much for us to consider. In particular, as I noted in chapter 1, we should enquire why the majority does not resist the minority, or even 'coerce' the minority into accepting instinctual pleasure; we should also enquire why the combined power of erotic ties does not prevail over the civilizing influence of society as a whole.

Firstly, then, we have to explain why a particular group, the minority, both favours the renunciation of instinctual pleasure and also is able to impose this on society: if this were not the case the institution of civilization would not be a stable institution. Freud touched on the question of motive in *Civilization and its Discontents*, suggesting the avoidance of pain as a motive.[11] He also touched on the question of opportunity, noting the necessity of this and suggesting that it arose from the power of an elite.[12] An explanation which is in the spirit of Freud's conjectures, and which involves both motive and opportunity, is based on sublimation. The anxiety associated with instinctual frustration may be dealt with in a variety of ways: some individuals fall prey to neurotic illness, others resort to sublimation, and yet others employ a range of alternative defences. But of these only sublimation, which is to be interpreted in this context in the specific sense of replacing feeling by thinking, is reasonably successful in avoiding pain. And only sublimation, harnessing as it does all the power of thinking, gives some degree of control over the environment. Thus those, and they typically constitute a minority, who resort predominantly to sublimation both have the motive and the opportunity to impose instinctual renunciation on society.

Secondly, we have to explain why, even if everyone prefers erotic ties (which, for the sake of argument, I shall now assume), society does not adopt an institutional structure based on such ties. Freud considered this question at some length. He noted that erotic ties essentially involve pairings, and that such pairings do not live easily with civilization: the pairings are antagonistic to civilization, since emotional energy is turned in to the relationship rather than out to civilization; and civilization is correspondingly antagonistic to pairings, tolerating them only when they benefit civilization, as in marriage.[13] It is within the spirit of Freud's observations, and consistent with the theory developed here, to suggest that the reason why society does not adopt an institutional structure based on erotic pairings, even when everyone prefers such pairings to civilization, is that such an institution would be unstable. As I showed in an earlier example (nominally involving religious denominations), pairings, however much desired, may be intrinsically unstable.

GROUPS AND SOCIETY

It is not difficult to re-interpret this example in terms of individuals and to extend it quite realistically in such a way as to suggest that an institution based on unrestricted pairings in society will be unstable.

The theoretical structure developed here is intended more as a framework in which to look at particular problems than as an explanation of the state of society in general. None the less, there would seem to be two general conclusions we may draw. Firstly, social arrangements are likely to be fragile: there may be no stable institutions, and if there are any then volatile group behaviour may disrupt them. Secondly, consensus is improbable: since aggression requires an enemy divisive institutions may dominate collusive ones. Indeed, we may combine these two conclusions in the hypothesis that the greater the consensus the greater the fragility: a consensus society with no one outside to project its hostile impulses into becomes overwhelmed by these impulses, psychotic, and volatile – in short, it becomes as an autistic child. If these conclusions appear pessimistic we might reflect that man has existed for over ten millennia with little evidence of periods of secure harmony, or even of movement in that direction.

The view of society which emerges is as a body whose elements are in a constant state of flux – as the electrons in an atom, or Leibniz's monads. At the heart of this flux is the basic interplay between group conflict and co-operation on which society so precariously rests. In terms of the behavioural theory, groups may co-operate at the unconscious level in achieving conflicting conscious behaviour, or indeed vice versa. In terms of the aggregation theory, groups form, or combine to create larger groups, in a co-operative way; and at the same time they divide, and split-off smaller groups, in a conflicting way. This concept of co-operation, that is, of combining and creating, is precisely that of the life instinct, Eros. And the concept of conflict, of dividing and destroying, is precisely that of the death instinct, thanatos.

Thus the theory developed here is, in spirit, remarkably similar to the essence of Freud's social theory, which I quoted briefly at the start of our enquiry, and which in more detail is summarized by Freud as follows.[14]

Civilization is a process in the service of Eros, whose purpose is to combine single human individuals, and after that families then races, peoples and nations, into one great unity, the unity of mankind. Why this has to happen, we do not know; the work of Eros is precisely this. These collections of men are to be libidinally bound to one another. Necessity alone, the advantages of work in common, will not hold them together. But man's natural aggressive instinct, the hostility of each against all and of all against each, opposes this programme of civilization. This aggressive instinct is the derivative and the main representative of the death instinct which we have found alongside of Eros and which shares world-dominion with it. And now, I think, the meaning of the evolution of civilization is no longer obscure to us: it must present the struggle between Eros and Death, between the instinct of life and the instinct of destruction, as it works itself out in the human species. This struggle is what all life essentially consists of, and the evolution of civilization may therefore be simply described as the struggle for life of the human species.

We have, then, by approaching the question from two directions not available to Freud, provided a more rigorous foundation for Freud's bold conjecture. The twin elements of this foundation are the behavioural theory and the aggregation theory. The former is based on psychoanalytical thinking of the independent school, and thus, as well as on the work of Freud, on that of Melanie Klein, much of which was developed only after Freud's death. The latter is based on social science, as originated by Adam Smith, with whose work Freud does not appear to have been familiar, and as developed in the paradigm of game theory, again after Freud's death. The nexus in which the two, psychoanalysis and social science, come together is the interplay between conflict and co-operation.

Appendix[15]

In this technical appendix I present more formally the theoretical model developed intuitively in this chapter.[16]

Let A be the set of possible institutions available to society and

GROUPS AND SOCIETY

N the set of individuals in society. Each individual in N has a preference ordering (over A), as defined in the appendix to chapter 4. Let M be the set of all possible groups, that is the set of non-empty subsets of N. Note that both singletons and N itself are elements of M; an element of M which is neither singleton nor N is a proper group.

The family of a group G in M comprises all non-empty sets of institutions which G can impose on society. The family is non-empty, since A is an element of the family of each G in M; and the family of N is equal to A. More generally, if F is a subgroup of G and U is an element of the family of F, then there is a non-empty subset V of U which is in the family of G.

If X and Y are two institutions in A, then Y dominates X if each individual in N prefers Y to X. As individual preferences are complete, asymmetric and transitive (as defined in the appendix to chapter 4), the dominance relation is also asymmetric and transitive, though is not complete. If an institution X in A is not dominated by any other institution in A then X is a *tenable* institution.

If A is finite then there exists some tenable institution. To see this take any institution in A and label it the top institution. Then take another institution; if this dominates the top institution then it replaces this as the new top institution. Repeat this process until A is exhausted. Then the final top institution is an undominated institution, and thus tenable. There may, however, be many tenable institutions: indeed, every institution in A may be tenable.

An institution X in A is dominated through a group G in M if there is some set S in the family of G such that, for each institution Y in S, each member of G prefers Y to X. If X is not dominated through any group in M then X is a *stable* institution.

Even if A is finite there may exist no stable institution, though it may be shown that stable institutions exist in a wide class of cases. On the other hand, every institution may be stable.

For simplicity of exposition I have not allowed for the possibility of an individual's preferences depending on the group of which he is a member. Provided that his preferences depend only on the members of the group, it is straightforward to incorporate

GROUPS AND SOCIETY

this possibility. It is also possible to allow for the preferences of each member of a group to depend on the preferences of other members, but this is more complex.

CHAPTER 6

Social attitudes

My main task in this book, the construction of a psychoanalytical theory of society, is now completed. That is to say, we now have a *general* theory relating the institutions adopted by society to the underlying aims of its members – general in the sense that the explanation is independent of what these aims may be.

I shall now, as an extension to the general theory, explore the nature of these individual aims in one central area: the so-called left-right dimension. In particular, I shall be concerned with the nature of the unconscious motives which underlie individuals' conscious left-right social attitudes.[1] (I use the term social rather than political because firstly, as we shall see, there is more to political attitudes than left-right ones; and secondly, I am not directly concerned with adherence to party doctrines – indeed, it is often more useful to consider political parties as groups of people with similar underlying social attitudes than to think of individuals choosing between political parties on the basis of party doctrines.)

Left-right attitudes particularly invite further investigation not only because they immediately concern our area of investigation, that is social institutions, but also because they are dominated by unconscious processes. As we saw in chapter 2, all thoughts develop out of phantasies through reality testing. Attitudes to our immediate circle – family, colleagues, lovers – may contain substantial elements of phantasy, but they are also

SOCIAL ATTITUDES

the subject of repeated reality testing through day-to-day contact; thus they gradually become modified to conform more closely, albeit not precisely, to (external) reality. On the other hand, our attitudes to politicians and to politics suffer relatively little reality testing, and accordingly remain dominated by unconscious phantasy. We rarely meet politicians, and when we do we tend to split the person from the politics – 'he is quite human underneath the left-wing (or right-wing) posturing.' And our great left or right ideals – the pure communist utopia or the stateless society of free individuals – never suffer the embarrassment of being confronted with reality.

One manifestation of this phantasy nature of left-right attitudes is that any exploration of the motives underlying them tends to be met with strong resistance. As Money-Kyrle has observed, 'the analyst who writes on political motives ... must be prepared to become the target of some hostilities.'[2] And, of course, the analyst himself is not immune. As Jones has confessed, 'analysts and other analysed persons often continue to hold heatedly the same convictions and to employ in support of them the same rationalised arguments as unanalysed people in such matters as political controversy: the sacrosanctity of private property and the capitalist system, or, on the other hand, the panacea of communism.'[3]

One of the basic aspects of left-right attitudes is that they tend to be polarized. Thus, to use two examples from political manifestos which I shall return to later, if someone is in favour of high levels of taxation it is likely that he will also be against fox hunting, although the two issues are apparently quite independent. This polarization reflects two processes. Firstly, when an individual shares some attitude with others he becomes a member of a group; as such he loses some of his own attitudes and takes in their place some of the attitudes of the group. This is the process of identification, which I discussed in chapter 4. Secondly, there may be consistent unconscious motives which underlie the apparently independent conscious ones – an aspect of the principle of mental continuity which I discussed in chapter 2. It is this second process which I explore in this chapter.

Although the dominant polarization of social attitudes is that

SOCIAL ATTITUDES

between left and right, there is at least one further significant polarization: that between the libertarian and the authoritarian. As these two dimensions are conceptually distinct the continuum of social attitudes may better be represented by a two-dimensional plane than by a one-dimensional line. (I shall later adduce some evidence for this two-dimensional picture, and also attach more precise meanings to these political labels.) We may thus, in principle, identify four distinct political groupings, even if their boundaries are somewhat fuzzy in practice. These four groupings, corresponding to the four quadrants of the plane, are the right-libertarian one of Adam Smith and the eighteenth-century liberals; the left-libertarian one of the Fabians and democratic socialism; the right-authoritarian one of feudalism and military dictatorships; and the left-authoritarian one of Stalinism and soviet-style communism.[4]

I shall concentrate on the left-right dimension for two reasons. Firstly, as I shall show, left-right attitudes are the direct residues of infantile anxieties: they originate in the ways in which the infant experienced and dealt with the paranoid and depressive positions. Libertarian-authoritarian attitudes, however, originate later, in the Oedipus crisis. They depend on the ways in which the child negotiates and resolves this crisis, authoritarian attitudes arising from a continuing unconscious identification with parental figures and libertarian ones from a continuing unconscious rebellion against such figures. Since, as I noted in chapter 3, the child deals with the Oedipus crisis using the various mechanisms he has learnt in infancy, that is, in the paranoid and depressive positions, the left-right dimension is in a sense more primitive than the libertarian-authoritarian one.

My second reason for concentrating on the left-right dimension is that, as I shall justify later, it is, at least in the democracies of the world, the dominant axis of political argument. The adoption of democracy has narrowed the range of libertarian-authoritarian options substantially, leaving the left-right axis as the main arena for dispute (or for the projection of internal conflicts): democracies have left-wing parties and right-wing parties, and even centre parties, but no explicitly and primarily libertarian or authoritarian parties.

SOCIAL ATTITUDES

Relatively little has been written on the unconscious motives underlying left-right attitudes. What has been written in this emotionally charged area is difficult to summarize faithfully; I shall therefore quote directly from some of the more relevant work.

Freud, and other members of his circle, made various passing references to political motives, but offered no systematic explanation. For example, in *Group Psychology* Freud interprets the desire for equality as follows.[5]

What appears later on in society in the shape of *Gemeingeist, esprit de corps* 'group spirit', etc., does not belie its derivation from what was originally envy. No one must want to put himself forward, every one must be the same and have the same. Social justice means that we deny ourselves many things so that others may have to do without them as well, or, what is the same thing, may not be able to ask for them. This demand for equality is the root of social conscience and the sense of duty. It reveals itself unexpectedly in the syphilitic's dread of infecting other people, which psycho-analysis has taught us to understand. The dread exhibited by these poor wretches corresponds to their violent struggles against the unconscious wish to spread their infection on to other people; for why should they alone be infected and cut off from so much? Why not other people as well? And the same germ is to be found in the apt story of the judgement of Solomon. If one woman's child is dead, the other shall not have a live one either. The bereaved woman is recognized by this wish.

This view contains an interesting germ, but is far from (and is not intended to be) a complete picture.

The first systematic explanation of social attitudes is that developed by Flugel in *Man, Morals and Society*. Flugel explains the root of political attitudes in the following terms.[6]

This lies in the parent-regarding, especially the father-regarding, attitude, and in the continuation of this attitude in introjected form in the super-ego; the 'right' or conservative attitude resulting from a predominance of, obedience to, admiration of, and identification with the parental figure or its substitutes in the external world or as introjected in the super-ego; the 'left' or radical attitude resulting from a rebellion against this figure, from an adoption of the child's standpoint as contrasted with that of the parent, of that of the ego as contrasted with that of the super-ego.

SOCIAL ATTITUDES

This view, despite the use of 'left' and 'right', is mainly concerned with the libertarian-authoritarian dimension, and particularly the root of this in the Oedipus crisis: libertarians unconsciously rebelling against parental figures and authoritarians unconsciously identifying with these. However, Flugel goes on to discuss ten more specific attributes in which left and right are distinguished.[7] I shall return to some of these traits later.

Flugel's ideas are developed by Money-Kyrle. In *Psychoanalysis and Politics* Money-Kyrle paints a stylized picture of two people, one an imaginary socialist and the other an imaginary conservative, albeit with the warning that neither should be regarded as typical of the parties, or opinions, which they support.[8]

The first is a single woman with no great desire or aptitude for marriage. She has had a hard struggle to make her way in life, but is now successfully established perhaps as a teacher or civil servant. If some Socratic sociologist were to examine the motives for her socialism he would begin by noticing her deep sympathy for those who are thwarted or deprived. So here at the outset he would find a humanistic motive which no analysis would undermine and which may therefore be expected to remain a constant determinant in her enthusiasm for a welfare state. But he may soon discover that her sympathy for the underprivileged is combined with a surprising degree of callousness or open hatred towards those who seem to her to be privileged too much. Then, if he pursued his questions further, he might well find that as a child she had been one of those girls who had desperately wanted to be a boy, that she had never outgrown her grievance, and that it was the unconscious source of her hatred of the overprivileged....

It is worth noting that among men, too, an unconscious sense of organic defect, when combined with economic deprivation, can lead to very much the same result – an intense hatred of those whose phallic superiority is suggested by such symbols as their streamlined cars, their old school ties, or their top hats.

Turning to the conservative – whom I repeat I do not choose as in any way typical of the party he supports – I will assume him to be a married man of independent means and a little over sensitive about his position as lord and master of his home. He is economically free to dispose of his life as and how he likes; and I will further suppose that he employs it in ways that he and those who know him best regard as useful and creative. To him freedom is the highest value, and he is therefore profoundly opposed to a regulated and bureaucratic state. All this seems rational enough. But his attitude to the other side is not. In his eyes, their sole aim is to deprive and thwart him and the class he belongs to. He can hardly credit them with any other motive, and cannot see that they are also, and perhaps even primarily, concerned to help those less favourably situated whose anxieties and troubles seem remote enough to him. Moreover, his fear and therefore his hatred is excessive. Threatened perhaps by some further cuts in income he feels himself in danger of utter destitution. A clue to his underlying motives is suggested by his attitude to his wife, and indeed to women in general. He only cares for those whom he feels to be 'feminine', by which he means seductive and submissive; and heartily dislikes those who enter what he regards as a masculine profession – especially if they are successful in it. Further inquiry into his early childhood would probably reveal one of those typical conflicts which so often end in a permanent, but unconscious, terror of castration. In his case, perhaps, an over anxious nurse may have really threatened him in an effort to stop an early tendency to masturbate; and he may have attributed her threat, not altogether without reason, to her envy of his masculine superiority. At any rate, this is the situation as it survives in his unconscious phantasy, which now influences his politics. To his unconscious, the socialists are a band of deprived and envious women whose sole aim is to castrate him. The first example will suggest that there may even be an element of truth in this unconscious picture. But it is one-sided and exaggerated.

These pictures contain some interesting conjectures (particularly the relevance of envy), but despite the disclaimer they are a little too specific and dominated by character traits to illustrate any general roots of left-right attitudes. In a later work Money-Kyrle suggests that unconscious feelings of envy are dominant in the deprived and unconscious feelings of guilt in the privileged.[9] And in a yet later paper he associates such guilt with both envy (again) and greed.[10]

Of various other writers touching on left-right attitudes, the most relevent is Meltzer. In *Sexual States of Mind* Meltzer identifies three different groups in the political population: 'rebels', who may be loosely identified with the left; 'conservatives', who may be loosely identified with the right; and 'revolutionaries', who (despite their name) have transcended politics.

SOCIAL ATTITUDES

Meltzer characterizes the states of mind of the first two of these groups as follows.[11]

Rebelliousness embraces all those states related to the height of the oedipus complex in which the struggle against the incest barrier is still in the forefront. It is characterised by contempt for the past, greed for power, resentment of authority, idealisation of novelty and disbelief in the importance of experience to the development of wisdom. It is dominated by persecutory anxiety and prone to violent means and the expectation of violent retaliation. It is determined to believe that the good people are being corrupted by the bad ones and that simple solutions and 'final solutions' require only 'courage', meaning ruthless destruction of enemies. Its aims therefore are always negatively stated, fallaciously argued and festooned with undocumented generalisation. Vendetta is the ethos and talion its rationale. Vital at 15, it becomes dangerously anti-social by 25.

Conservatism is the state of mind resulting from regression to latency mechanisms in the face of adult responsibility and the depressive task of working through the oedipus complex and accepting commitment to introjective identification with a combined object. Its longing for stability at any price inclines it to sacrifice growth and development just as it sacrifices sexual passion to comfort. Being the product of introjective and/or projective identification with separated and de-sexualised objects, it is envious of youth, prone to equate age automatically with experience and therefore with wisdom. The belief in omnipotent control and balancing techniques inclines it to bargaining and compromise, while impaired symbol formation and constricted imagination render it at once materialistic, acquisitive and prone to confuse social roles with whole people. Its respect for titles and offices is therefore automatic, subject only to 'checks and balances'. Being unable to distinguish novelty from originality, it leans heavily on tradition to save it from confusion of values. Its denial of psychic reality impels it to see all events as 'cause and effect' while even simple cyclic problems such as 'chicken and egg' are viewed as mischievous word-twisting. It disbelieves the history of its own rebelliousness, for it has disavowed that identity and its unique development.

This view contains some interesting germs (particularly the relevance of omnipotence). However, although it relates in passing to left-right activities it is more concerned with libertarian-authoritarian ones and the roots of these in the Oedipus crisis, particularly as they are manifest in Meltzer's main concern of

SOCIAL ATTITUDES

intergenerational conflict and permanent revolution.

Before exploring the unconscious motives which underlie left-wing and right-wing attitudes I shall attempt to identify the essential aspects of such attitudes. Clearly this cannot be done with any precision, since both left and right attitudes are quite diverse. Not only do they meet in the centre, but they also complete the circle, as it were, at their extremes: anarchism may be interpreted either as a far left position or as a far right one. Also, left-right attitudes are not completely independent of libertarian-authoritarian ones, despite our two-dimensional idealization. None the less, there do seem to be some social attitudes which are of the essence of the left and some which are of the essence of the right.

It is useful to identify left and right attitudes both by their aims and by their means, though naturally the two are not independent. Left and right are not symmetric in this: the left emphasizes 'aims' while taking 'means' as secondary, while the right emphasizes 'means' while taking 'aims' as secondary.

The right emphasizes the means of 'competition' and individual independence, of allowing individuals to pursue their own goals with little interference or support from society. The corresponding aim is 'efficiency', that is, obtaining as large a cake as possible irrespective of the sizes of the slices. These aims and means are linked by the philosophy of Adam Smith's invisible hand, that the interest of society is best served by the self-interest of individuals. Thus what the right wants most from society is that it be bountiful, munificent and productive. And it sees society as being inherently Darwinian and competitive: sometimes this is accepted regretfully, with resignation, and sometimes aggressively, as a challenge.

The left, on the other hand, emphasizes the aim of 'equity', that is, obtaining a fair (usually equal) division of the cake into slices irrespective of the size of the whole cake. The means by which this is to be achieved is that of 'collaboration' and collective organization, of making the individual directly responsible to society. The only philosophy which is required to link these aims and means is the recognition that competition does not

SOCIAL ATTITUDES

achieve equity. Thus what the left wants most from society is that it be fair, decent and just. And it sees society as being, at best, comradely and collaborative: if it is not so now this discrepancy may be seen as being due either to temporary problems of transition or to oppression by an elite.

In summary, then, attitudes of the right may be characterized by efficiency and competition, and those of the left by equity and collaboration. This gives us two aspects of the left-right dimension: that concerning efficiency versus equity, and that concerning competition versus collaboration. I shall, in due course, consider each of these separately, relating attitudes on efficiency versus equity to the paranoid position, and those on competition versus collaboration to the depressive position.

Firstly, however, I shall illustrate these somewhat abstract principles (and also provide some justification for concentrating on left-right attitudes) with the evidence on political attitudes in England in the 1970s obtained by Hilde Himmelweit and others.[12]

The authors ask people to evaluate a number of issues. One of their central conclusions from the responses they receive is that attitudes are closely clustered along two dimensions, or, as they put it, clearly fall into one of two 'supra-families'.[13]

> Families of attitudes grouped within the first major family ... concern class or economic issues: public ownership (of building land, companies; abolition of private health service, etc.), trade unions (their powers; can they be trusted? are they harmful?), strikes (the need for legal sanctions; social security benefits to strikers, etc.), big business (should it be controlled, more heavily taxed, etc?). They also include attitudes to selective secondary schooling.

> Families of attitudes grouped within the second supra-family ... concern law and order, the need for stricter laws and increase in the power of the police, etc., views on capital punishment and the law on homosexuality as well as on immigration (should it be restricted? should it be controlled on the basis of colour, etc?).

The first of these supra-families clearly corresponds to the left-right dimension and the second to the libertarian-authoritarian.

Our concern, the left-right dimension, is illustrated by a list of

SOCIAL ATTITUDES

twenty-one issues each evaluated by people with one of three party allegiances: Labour, which I shall, loosely at least, identify with the left; Conservative, identified with the right; and Liberal, allocated to the centre.[14] (It is of course an approximation to identify Labour with the left, Conservatives with the right and Liberals with the centre, and one which would be resented by many activists; this should be borne in mind in what follows.) I have arbitrarily expressed the issues (by including a '*not*' if appropriate) in a way such that they are supported by the left and opposed by the right, though of course the phrasing, and subsequent comments, can be reversed. I have ranked the issues according to the difference between the average left and right evaluations, so that issues at the top of the list are more contentious than those at the bottom.

Nationalize building land
Nationalize companies
Abolish grammar schools
Not allow private health care
Not cut benefits to strikers
Increase taxes on wealthy
Not sell council houses to tenants
Trust trade unions
Subsidize foods
Not stay in EEC
Not cut taxes on companies
Not control wage rises
Enforce equal pay for women
Spend more on social services
Encourage worker participation
Stop unemployment rising
Not encourage repatriation of immigrants
Not control mortgage rate rises
Restrict price rises
Not make industry more efficient
Not reform electoral system

All the most divisive issues, say the top quarter of the list, embody both equity and collaboration (as opposed to efficiency and competition, since issues are expressed as being supported by the left and opposed by the right). For example, nationalizing

115

SOCIAL ATTITUDES

building land and companies both ensures that the gains from development and profits of companies are shared amongst all, and also breaks down the division between 'them' (the owners and shareholders) and 'us' (the residents and employees). The next most divisive issues, the second quarter of the list, embody either equity or collaboration, but in no case either efficiency or competition. For example, increasing taxes on the wealthy is mainly concerned with equity, with sharing the spoils of the rich, though also has some overtones of collaboration. And trusting trade unions is mainly concerned with collaboration, with labour and capital working in harmony, though also has some overtones of equity. Thus the characterization of the left-right dimension as being that of equity and collaboration on the one hand versus efficiency and competition on the other has some justification.

A further implication of this list of issues is that the left-right dimension is indeed more important than the libertarian-authoritarian one. Almost all of the issues in the top half of the list are characterized by the authors as belonging to their first supra-family, that is, to the left-right dimension, and almost all of those in the bottom half are characterized as belonging to the second (libertarian-authoritarian) family.

It is also interesting to note that centrists are indeed in the centre of the left-right continuum rather than on some different plane. For almost all issues the average centrist evaluation lies between the average left and right evaluations, the few exceptions all being in the bottom quarter of the list.

Given this characterization of the attitudes of the right by efficiency and competition and of those of the left by equity and collaboration, I now turn to the roots of these adult social attitudes in the life of the infant. As I have suggested, attitudes on efficiency versus equity may be related to developments in the paranoid position, and attitudes on competition versus collaboration to developments in the depressive position. As I discussed in chapter 3, the adult continually reverts to the mechanisms of these positions, and the anxieties he experiences and defences he employs are dominated by those he first experi-

SOCIAL ATTITUDES

enced and employed as an infant. Thus our adult social attitudes are expressions of quite unconscious infantile mechanisms. (They are also, of course, expressions of conscious rational processes; my purpose is not to deny conscious explanations of social attitudes, but to add to these.)

I shall start with the earlier paranoid position, and explore the connection between a desire for efficiency and a preponderance of unconscious greed on the one hand, and that between a desire for equity and a preponderance of unconscious envy on the other. Greed and envy may be seen as manifestations of the life and death instincts in the paranoid position. Greed is the impulse to grab and possess all the goodness of an object, quite regardless of any possible harm to or destruction of the object. Being concerned with obtaining goodness it is thus a manifestation, albeit disturbed, of the life instinct. Envy, on the other hand, is the impulse to spoil and destroy a good object, regardless of any possible gain from or possession of its goodness. It is then a clear, and indeed first, externalization of the death instinct.

The significance of these emotions, and the distinction between them and jealousy, is elaborated by Melanie Klein in *Envy and Gratitude* in the following terms.[15]

A distinction should be drawn between envy, jealousy, and greed. Envy is the angry feeling that another person possesses and enjoys something desirable – the envious impulse being to take it away or to spoil it. Moreover, envy implies the subject's relation to one person only and goes back to the earliest exclusive relation with the mother. Jealousy is based on envy, but involves a relation to at least two people; it is mainly concerned with love that the subject feels is his due and has been taken away, or is in danger of being taken away, from him by his rival. In the everyday conception of jealousy, a man or a woman feels deprived of the loved person by somebody else.

Greed is an impetuous and insatiable craving, exceeding what the subject needs and what the object is able and willing to give. At the unconscious level, greed aims primarily at completely scooping out, sucking dry, and devouring the breast: that is to say, its aim is destructive introjection; whereas envy not only seeks to rob in this way, but also to put badness, primarily bad excrements and bad parts of self, into the mother, and first of all into her breast, in order to spoil and destroy her. In the deepest sense this means destroying her creativeness.

SOCIAL ATTITUDES

This process, which derives from urethral- and anal-sadistic impulses, I have elsewhere defined as a destructive aspect of projective identification starting from the beginning of life. One essential difference between greed and envy, although no rigid dividing line can be drawn since they are so closely associated, would accordingly be that greed is mainly bound up with introjection and envy with projection . . . .

It could be said that the very envious person is insatiable, he can never be satisfied because his envy stems from within and therefore always finds an object to focus on. This shows also the close connection between jealousy, greed and envy.

Melanie Klein goes on to discuss the origins of these emotions in the paranoid position of infancy as follows.[16]

I have often described the sadistic attacks on the mother's breast as determined by destructive impulses. Here I wish to add that envy gives particular impetus to these attacks. This means that when I wrote about the greedy scooping out of the breast and of the mother's body, and the destruction of her babies, as well as putting bad excrements into the mother, this adumbrated what I later came to recognize as the envious spoiling of the object.

If we consider that deprivation increases greed and persecutory anxiety, and that there is in the infant's mind a phantasy of an inexhaustible breast which is his greatest desire, it becomes understandable how envy arises even if the baby is adequately fed. The infant's feelings seem to be that when the breast deprives him, it becomes bad because it keeps the milk, love, and care associated with the good breast all to itself. He hates and envies what he feels to be the mean and grudging breast.

It is perhaps more understandable that the satisfactory breast is also envied. The very ease with which the milk comes – though the infant feels gratified by it – also gives rise to envy because this gift seems something unattainable.

These quotations directly demonstrate a clear identification between efficiency, or obtaining as large a cake as possible, and unconscious greed. Wanting an ever-bigger cake, all that can be obtained, is (in addition to its quite rational aspects) an almost direct manifestation of 'an impetuous and insatiable craving', of 'completely scooping out, sucking dry, and devouring the breast'. On the other hand, this only involves envy peripherally, if at all.

There is also a clear identification between equity, or obtaining a fair division of the cake, and envy, since any redistribution necessarily involves (both logically and emotionally, as the quotation from *Group Psychology* earlier in this chapter shows) reducing the slices of someone. Feeling that someone has too large a slice, and wanting to take some of it from him, is (again in addition to its quite rational aspects) an almost direct expression of 'the angry feeling that another person possesses and enjoys something desirable', the 'impulse being to take it away'. On the other hand, this only involves greed peripherally, if at all.

I now turn to the later depressive position, and explore the connection between a competitive view of society and a predominance of omnipotent defences on the one hand, and that between a collaborative view of society and a predominance of manic reparation on the other. Omnipotent defences and manic reparation are alternative reactions to feelings of mourning and guilt in the depressive position. Omnipotent defences involve denying the dependence on the object; they typically take the form of a mixture of triumph, that is, denying the power of the object, and contempt, that is denying the importance and value of the object. Manic reparation, on the other hand, attempts to restore the object without feeling any guilt. This is typically achieved by ensuring that although the object is seen as being injured it is not seen as having been injured by oneself, and, because it is injured, seeing it as inferior.

The significance of omnipotent, or manic, defences is elaborated by Melanie Klein;[17] her views are summarized by Hanna Segal in the following terms.[18]

> Denial of psychic reality can be maintained by the re-awakening and strengthening of omnipotence and particularly of omnipotent control of the object.
>
> The manic relation to objects is characterized by a triad of feelings – control, triumph and contempt. These feelings are directly related to, and defensive against depressive feelings of valuing the object and depending on it, and fear of loss and guilt. Control is a way of denying dependence, of not acknowledging it and yet of compelling the object to fulfil a need for dependence, since an object that is wholly controlled is,

SOCIAL ATTITUDES

up to a point, one that can be depended on. Triumph is a denial of depressive feelings of valuing and caring; it is linked with omnipotence and has two important aspects. One is connected with the primary attack made on the object in the depressive position, and with the triumph experienced in defeating this object, particularly if the attack is strongly determined by envy. Secondarily, the feeling of triumph is increased as part of the manic defences, because it keeps at bay those depressive feelings which would otherwise be aroused, such as pining and longing for and missing the object. Contempt for the object is again a direct denial of valuing the object, which is so important in the depressive position, and it acts as a defence against the experience of loss and guilt. An object of contempt is not an object worthy of guilt, and the contempt that is experienced in relation to such an object becomes a justification for further attacks on it.

Melanie Klein also discusses the significance of manic reparation;[19] Hanna Segal summarizes this discussion as follows.[20]

Manic reparation is a defence in that its aim is to repair the object in such a way that guilt and loss are never experienced. An essential feature of manic reparation is that it has to be done without acknowledgement of guilt, and therefore under special conditions. For instance, manic reparation is never done in relation to primary objects or internal objects, but always in relation to more remote objects; secondly, the object in relation to which reparation is done must never be experienced as having been damaged by oneself; thirdly, the object must be felt as inferior, dependent and, at depth, contemptible. There can be no true love or esteem for the object or objects that are being repaired, as this would threaten the return of true depressive feelings. Manic reparation can never be completed, because, if it were complete, the object fully restored would again become lovable and esteemed, and free from the manic person's omnipotent control and contempt. Fully restored to independence and again endowed with value, it would be exposed once more to immediate attack with hatred and contempt.

Because of these conditions, the underlying guilt which manic reparation seeks to alleviate is, in fact, not relieved, and the reparation brings no lasting satisfaction. The objects that are being repaired are unconsciously, and sometimes consciously, treated with hatred and contempt and are invariably felt as ungrateful and, at least unconsciously, are dreaded as potential persecutors.

One can sometimes see this kind of manic reparation in charitable institutions, when, for instance, those in control see themselves as spending charity and reparation on unworthy and ungrateful people whom they feel to be essentially bad and dangerous.

These quotations directly demonstrate a clear identification between a competitive Darwinian view of the world and omnipotent defences. The individualistic law of the jungle is a direct embodiment of triumph over, and contempt for, those who fall by the wayside. And there is also a clear identification between a comradely and collaborative view of the world and manic reparation. As we are all one large happy family we cannot have damaged anyone; further, no one will rise above us and 'be exposed once more to immediate attack'.

Finally, it remains to consider the connection between unconscious envy and manic reparation (both of which are associated with attitudes of the left), and that between unconscious greed and omnipotent defences (both of which are associated with attitudes of the right).

Firstly, there is at least some connection between envy and manic reparation. It is an aim of manic reparation to ensure that the object is never fully restored, lovable and esteemed, which aim is but a milder version of the spoiling and destroying sought by envy. Greed, however, would be well satisfied by a fully restored object, for it would then be an object worth scooping out and sucking dry. Secondly, there is also some connection between greed and omnipotent defences. It is an aim of omnipotent defences to control the object so that it can be depended on, and depended on to yield up its goodness. Envy, however, would be far from satisfied by a dependable object, whose dependability it would need to destroy.

But these connections are not complete, and should not be exaggerated. We should expect to find a tendency for unconscious envy to be accompanied by manic reparation, jointly manifest in unambiguous left-wing attitudes; and also a tendency for unconscious greed to be accompanied by omnipotent defences, jointly manifest in unambiguous right-wing attitudes. But we should also expect to find some cases of envy accompanied by omnipotent defences, and of greed accompanied by

SOCIAL ATTITUDES

manic reparation, both of which combinations being manifest in more centrist attitudes.

I shall illustrate this interpretation of left and right attitudes with some material from some recent manifestos, those for the 1983 general election, of the two main English political parties. In so doing I shall continue, again as an approximation, to identify the Labour Party with the left and the Conservative Party with the right.

As might be expected, each party's manifesto attempts to be all things to all men, and is thus somewhat bland. The material I shall consider is deliberately selective: it is chosen to illustrate the occasional irruptions of emotion rather than the carefully groomed and unobjectionable surface. (One of the more interesting examples of such, which in fact occurs in a manifesto for the preceding election, is the right's intuitive observation that the left had been 'practising the politics of envy';[21] the left seems to have had no corresponding insight into the politics of greed.)

The material I shall consider falls into four areas: economic, foreign, social and sporting. In the first of these I am concerned with the central question of redistribution: whether the tax system is to be used to 'soak the rich' or to 'let people keep all they can get their hands on'. From the left:[22]

> We shall reform taxation so that the rich pay their full share./ Capital taxes will be used to reduce the huge inequalities in wealth. We shall reverse most of the Tories' concessions on capital transfer tax and introduce a new annual tax on wealth./ This will ensure that the richest 100,000 of the population make a fair and proper contribution.

And from the right:[23]

> We have: cut the basic rate of income tax;/ brought the higher rates of income tax down; cut business taxes./ This dramatic programme is all the more striking when compared with the vast increase in taxation which our opponents' policies would inevitably bring.

The interpretation of the left viewpoint depends, at least in emphasis, on whether the person expressing it is relatively wealthy or not (holding left-wing views does not, of course, preclude the holding of wealth). For those who have little wealth the left view, particularly with its emphasis on taking from the

SOCIAL ATTITUDES

rich rather than giving to the poor, is an expression of unconscious envy, that 'another person possesses and enjoys something desirable – the impulse being to take it away'. For the relatively wealthy the left view is more an expression of token, or manic, reparation, which 'is never done in relation to primary objects or internal objects, but always in relation to more remote objects' – the abstract poor. The interpretation of the right view, on the other hand, depends less on the station of the person expressing it. It is an expression both of unconscious greed, of 'completely scooping out', and of manic defences such as triumph, 'a denial of depressive feelings of valuing and caring'.

In the second area I shall consider the dual response to foreigners and their products. Broadly speaking, the left-wing response is to impose controls on imports but allow free immigration, while the right-wing response is to allow free trade but restrict immigration. Thus for the left:[24]

We must therefore be ready to act on imports *directly:*/ we will ... introduce back-up import controls, using tariffs and quotas./ We will repeal [two Conservative Acts] and replace them with a citizenship law that does not discriminate.

And for the right:[25]

We are playing a leading part in preserving an open world trading system./ To have good community relations we have to maintain efficient immigration control.

In the left-wing position import controls are (amongst other things) an expression of unconscious envy of foreigners for having 'unfair' advantages such as 'cheap' labour, while free immigration fosters the phantasy of one harmonious international brotherhood of man. In the right-wing position free trade is (amongst other things) an expression of greed, of wanting to get as much as possible at as little cost as possible, while immigration restrictions are a response to the phantasy of ruthless invasion, of 'foreigners taking our jobs'. A further aspect of these dual left and right responses which we might note in passing is that they are experienced as being markedly different, a major facet of the distinction between left and right. But in reality they are remarkably similar: there is not very

SOCIAL ATTITUDES

much to choose between excluding the labour of the foreigner and excluding the fruits of his labour.

In the social area I shall use the examples of housing, health and education. Here, the left-wing view is that such services should typically be both provided and allocated by the state, while the right-wing view is that they should typically be provided through the profit motive and allocated according to ability to pay. Thus the left view:[26]

Labour will ... empower public landlords to repurchase homes sold under the Tories./ The present expansion in private medicine is a serious threat to our priorities in health care. We will not allow the development of a two-tier health service, where the rich can jump the queue./ *Private schools* are a major obstacle to a free and fair education system./ We shall also withdraw charitable status from private schools and all their other public subsidies and privileges.

And the right:[27]

We have given every council and New Town tenant the legal right to buy his or her home;/ a labour government would take away the tenant's right to buy his council house./ We welcome the growth in private health insurance;/ we shall continue to encourage this./ We shall defend Church schools and independent schools alike against our opponents' attacks. And we shall defend the right of parents to spend their own money on education.

Here again the left view embodies a mixture of unconscious envy of anyone who might be able to obtain better housing, health care or education than others with the phantasy that we are all one happy family sharing these services. And the right view embodies a mixture of unconscious greed for as much as possible of these services with the triumphant view that others can do without.

Finally, and perhaps most interestingly simply because it is apparently so peripheral, is sport. For the left:[28]

Fox hunting and all forms of hunting with dogs will be made illegal. This will not, however, affect shooting and fishing.

And for the right, albeit a little more generally:[29]

SOCIAL ATTITUDES

It is not for the Government to try to dictate how men and women should organise their lives.

The left is enraged by the phantasy of an elite unspeakable in pursuit of the uneatable, though not apparently out of concern for the latter, whose cousins may be shot or caught with impunity; while the right, discreetly, revels in the idea.

I shall conclude this investigation into social attitudes with a deliberately speculative exploration of the roots of various character traits which are often perceived as being associated with either left or right attitudes, even though they have little or no obvious connections with equity or collaboration on the one hand or with efficiency or competition on the other. The object of this exploration is not to suggest that the character trait determines the political attitude, or indeed that the political attitude determines the character trait; it is instead to suggest that both the political attitude and the character trait are, in their own different ways, expressions of underlying unconscious attributes such as envy or greed. This provides hypotheses which, at least in principle, may be tested. A weakness in identifying, for example, right-wing attitudes with an underlying unconscious greed is that although the former can be observed the latter, by its very nature, cannot. However, if we suggest that right-wing attitudes tend to be associated with sexual jealousy we have a hypothesis which, at least in principle, has some observable implications.

This is, of course, dangerous territory, since character traits are only somewhat loosely identified with left-right attitudes. Even if sexual jealousy is typically a trait of the right there will be many on the right who are relatively free from this emotion as well as many on the left who are its slave. Also, the character traits I explore are not intended to be comprehensive; indeed, they are deliberately quite selective.

The traits I consider are manifestations of some of the attributes proposed by Flugel as distinguishing left from right.[30] Flugel lists ten such distinguishing attitudes. Six of these, which need not detain us, are fairly direct expressions of equity versus efficiency or collaboration versus competition. The relevant

SOCIAL ATTITUDES

aspects of the remainder, which are less direct expressions of this divide and which I shall consider, are leadership acceptance, class antagonism, female homosexuality and sexual jealousy.

I shall concentrate on the manifestations of unconscious envy and greed, rather than those of manic reparation and omnipotent defences, since the former tend to be expressed on a wider and less directly political front than the latter. Also, to avoid repetition, or more accurately to avoid following each argument by its obverse, I shall concentrate on the connections between typically left forms of the various traits and unconscious envy; but the argument could just as well be expressed in terms of the connection between typically right forms and unconscious greed.

Firstly, then, the politics of the left (not to mention those of the psychoanalytic movement) are typified by quite open struggles between factions and the general failure to accept the authority of any one leader. The right, on the other hand, stands much more defensively behind its leader, and accordingly engages only more covertly in factional struggles. For example, Skynner and Cleese (under the appropriate heading of 'Paranoia and Politics') identify some fifty parties on the far left in England, over twice as many as on the far right.[31] Now loyalty to a leader is the result of identification with the leader, and party homogeneity is the result of these common identifications by party members. One of the effects of unconscious envy, though not of greed, is that identification is interfered with. Melanie Klein traces this process as follows.[32]

> Excessive envy, an expression of destructive impulses, interferes with the primal split between good and bad breast, and the building up of a good object cannot sufficiently be achieved ... [but] if the good object is deeply rooted ... identification with a good and whole object is the more securely established.

Thus unconscious envy, involving as it does some failure of identification, may be associated with a lack of leadership acceptance as well as with left-wing attitudes.

Secondly, the left is typically hostile to, and the right admiring of, the more upper classes in society. The hostility of the left involves not only the wish to take away the privileges of such classes, but also the wish to devalue: not only should their property be expropriated, but also they themselves are denigrated. One of the main defences against envy is devaluation. As Melanie Klein notes, 'defence against envy often takes the form of *devaluation of the object*; ... the object which has been devalued need not be envied any more'.[33] Thus envy, through devaluation, is associated with class antagonism as well as with left-wing attitudes.

Thirdly, many lesbian women have identified with the left, in contrast with gay men; or at least female homosexuals tend to be to the left of male while women as a whole are not noticeably to the left of men. One of the roots of female homosexuality lies in envy, as Melanie Klein shows.[34]

The penis is strongly equated with the breast (Abraham) and in my experience the woman's penis-envy can be traced back to envy of the mother's breast .... When envy of the mother's breast has been strongly transferred to the father's penis, the outcome may be a reinforcing of her homosexual attitude.

There are, of course, other roots of homosexuality in both women and men, but this root in envy is relevant only to women, and thus constitutes a link between female homosexuality and left-wing political views.

Finally, sexual jealousy is often perceived as belonging more to the right than to the left, in that the right tends to be more possessive in sexual relations and the left more sharing. As Melanie Klein notes,[35] 'if envy is not excessive, jealousy in the Oedipus situation becomes a means of working it through.' Thus jealousy may loosely be identified with an absence of envy. (More directly, jealousy is identified with greed since a greedy person wants all there is of the object and cannot tolerate any sharing of it with another.)

In these examples a consistent pattern is apparent: left-wing political attitudes and the form of the character trait more typical of the left are associated with one another through having a common root in unconscious envy. And, as I have emphasized, obverse arguments may be made associating right-wing political attitudes with the right form of the character trait through a common root in unconscious greed. But, I would

SOCIAL ATTITUDES

emphasize, these connections are not complete and should not be exaggerated.

In summary, then, left-wing attitudes are a manifestation of unconscious envy and manic reparation, while right-wing attitudes are a manifestation of unconscious greed and omnipotent defences. Common to both left and right is the attempt to work through internal conflicts by projecting them into the political arena and dealing with them externally. But what of the happy (even if imaginary) individual who has worked through the paranoid position free from both envy and greed, and who has come to terms with the anxiety of the depressive position through genuine reparation rather than manic reparation or omnipotent defences? He is neither of the left nor the right, nor indeed of the centre: he works through his internal conflicts internally instead of externalizing them in the political, or any other, arena.

The disadvantages of attempting to deal with internal conflicts externally are twofold. Firstly, it is a grossly inefficient use of emotional energy, in that energy is directed at the apparent problem rather than at the real problem. And secondly, by its nature it must involve, use, manipulate, and ultimately exploit, others. The first harms the individual, the second harms society. I have thus far refrained from any suggestions for social improvement. (Like Freud,[36] I hope I may say that 'I have no knowledge of having had any craving in my early childhood to help suffering humanity; my innate sadistic disposition was not a very strong one, so that I had no need to develop this one of its derivatives'.) But in conclusion I shall allow myself one prescriptive observation – one which brings us back to the invisible hand. The genuine way for the individual to benefit society, as well as himself and those around him, is for him to attempt to work through his internal conflicts internally rather than externally. Or, more simply, charity begins at home.

Notes

Abbreviations

SE   J. Strachey, A. Freud, A. Strachey and A. Tyson (eds), *The Standard Edition of the Complete Psychological Works of Sigmund Freud*, Hogarth Press, London, 1953–74 (24 vols).

W   R. Money-Kyrle, B. Joseph, E. O'Shaughnessy and H. Segal (eds), *The Writings of Melanie Klein*, Hogarth Press, London, 1975 (3 vols).

Chapter 1 The structure of society

1. A. Smith, *An Enquiry into the Nature and Causes of the Wealth of Nations*, Clarendon Press, Oxford, 1976, vol. 1, p. 456.
2. *SE*, vol. 21, p. 122.
3. *Matthew*, ch. 22, vv. 37–40.
4. Henceforth, 'his' (etc.) is used in the generic sense for 'his or her' (etc.) unless the context indicates otherwise.
5. *SE*, vol. 20, p. 69.
6. *SE*, vol. 21, p. 6.
7. *SE*, vol. 21, p. 86.
8. F. de Saussure, *Course in General Linguistics*, Collins, London, 1974, p. 81.
9. F. Kermode, 'Freud and interpretation', *The International Review of Psycho-Analysis*, 1985, vol. 12, pp. 3–12.

10 *SE*, vol. 13, pp. 157–8.
11 *SE*, vol. 13, p. xiii.
12 *SE*, vol. 18, p. 70.
13 *SE*, vol. 18, pp. 257–8.
14 *SE*, vol. 23, p. 132.
15 W. R. Bion, *Experiences in Groups and other Papers*, Tavistock, London, 1961, p. 168.
16 E. Fromm, *The Fear of Freedom*, Routledge & Kegan Paul, London, 1942, pp. 7–9.
17 Ibid., p. 10.
18 K. Marx, *Economic and Philosophic Manuscripts of 1844*, Progress Publishers, Moscow, 1959, p. 99.
19 *SE*, vol. 13, pp. 100–61.
20 *SE*, vol. 21, pp. 5–56.

Chapter 2 The individual mind

1 Some of the material from which this discussion is drawn is summarized in the works referred to in note 6 of this chapter.
2 *SE*, vol. 5, p. 608.
3 *SE*, vol. 14, p. 16.
4 Letter to H. G. Wells, quoted in J. Harrisson, 'The Freud Museum, London', *The International Review of Psycho-Analysis*, vol. 13, 1986, p. 255.
5 Letter to E. Jones, quoted in P. Grosskurth, *Melanie Klein*, Hodder & Stoughton, London, 1985, p. 161.
6 The views of the classical group are abridged in A. Freud (ed.), *The Essentials of Psycho-Analysis*, Hogarth Press, London, 1986; and those of the Kleinian group in J. Mitchell (ed.), *The Selected Melanie Klein*, Penguin, Harmondsworth, 1986. A representative exposition of some independent views is contained in G. Kohon (ed.), *The British School of Psychoanalysis*, Free Association Books, London, 1986.
7 A warning: the writer's analyst was of this group, and indeed an analytical grandson of both Sigmund Freud and Melanie Klein.
8 *SE*, vol. 7, pp. 125–248.
9 *SE*, vol. 18, pp. 3–66.
10 *SE*, vol. 5, pp. 509–622.
11 *SE*, vol. 19, pp. 3–68.

12   A. Freud, *The Ego and the Mechanisms of Defence*, Hogarth Press, London, 1937.
13   W. R. Bion, *Learning from Experience*, Heinemann, London, 1962.

Chapter 3 Individual development

1   Some of the material from which this discussion is drawn is summarized in the works referred to in note 6 of chapter 2.
2   H. Segal, *Introduction to the Work of Melanie Klein*, Hogarth Press, London, 1973, pp. 31–4.
3   Ibid., pp. 70–2.
4   E. Jaques, 'Death and the mid-life crisis', *The International Journal of Psycho-Analysis*, vol. 46, 1965, p. 506.
5   H. Ellis, 'The analysis of the sexual impulse', *The Alienist and Neurologist*, vol. 21, 1900, p. 250.
6   B. Bettelheim, *Freud and Man's Soul*, Hogarth Press, London, 1983.
7   *SE*, vol. 21, p. 43.

Chapter 4 Individuals and the group

1   The discussion draws on Freud's *Group Psychology* (*SE*, vol. 18, pp. 69–145); W. R. Bion, *Experience in Groups and other Papers*, Tavistock, London, 1961; and E. Jaques, 'Social systems as a defence against persecutory and depressive anxiety', in M. Klein, P. Heimann and R. E. Money-Kyrle (eds), *New Directions in Psycho-Analysis*, Tavistock, London, 1955, pp. 478–98.
2   A. N. Whitehead and B. Russell, *Principia Mathematica*, Cambridge University Press, Cambridge, 1967, pp. 37–65.
3   *SE*, vol. 18, pp. 69–145.
4   B. Bettelheim, *Freud and Man's Soul*, Hogarth Press, London, 1983.
5   G. le Bon, *The Crowd*, Benn, London, 1947, pp. 41–77.
6   Bion, op.cit., pp. 61–3.
7   W. Trotter, *Instincts of the Herd in Peace and War*, Unwin, London, 1919, pp. 105–10.
8   *SE*, vol. 14, pp. 87–90.
9   A. K. Rice, *Learning for Leadership*, Tavistock, London, 1965.

NOTES TO PAGES 65–107

10 I. E. P. Menzies, *The Functioning of Social Systems as a Defence against Anxiety*, Tavistock Pamphlets, London, 1970.
11 Jaques, op.cit., pp. 487–95.
12 This appendix may be omitted without loss of continuity.
13 This result is a version of a theorem due to K. J. Arrow, *Social Choice and Individual Values*, Wiley, New York, 1951.

Chapter 5 Groups and society

1 W. R. Bion, *Experiences in Groups and Other Papers*, Tavistock, London, 1961, p. 50.
2 J. O. Wisdom, 'Types of groups', *The International Review of Psycho-Analysis*, 1985, vol. 12, pp. 80–1; I have simplified the notation in this quotation.
3 *SE*, vol. 22, pp. 199–218.
4 F. Y. Edgeworth, *Mathematical Psychics*, Kegan Paul, London, 1881.
5 V. Pareto, *Manual of Political Economy*, Macmillan, London, 1972.
6 This discussion draws on M. Allingham, *Value*, Macmillan, London, 1983.
7 See, for example, ibid., pp. 32–40.
8 *W*, vol. 3, pp. 202–3.
9 *SE*, vol. 13, pp. 100–61.
10 *SE*, vol. 21, pp. 5–56.
11 *SE*, vol. 21, p. 26.
12 *SE*, vol. 21, pp. 5–9.
13 *SE*, vol. 21, pp. 99–105.
14 *SE*, vol. 21, p. 120.
15 This appendix may be omitted without loss of continuity.
16 This model involves a generalization of the concept of the core, which in turn is due to H. Scarf, 'An analysis of markets with a large number of participants', in M. Maschler (ed.), *Recent Advances in Game Theory*, Princeton University Press, Princeton, 1962, pp. 127–55.

Chapter 6 Social attitudes

1 The discussion draws on M. Allingham, 'Envy, greed, and political attitude', *The Journal of the Melanie Klein Society*, vol. 4, 1986, pp. 131–40.

2   R. E. Money-Kyrle, *Psychoanalysis and Politics*, Duckworth, London, 1951.
3   E. Jones, 'The concept of a normal mind', *The International Journal of Psycho-Analysis*, vol. 23, 1942, p. 4.
4   A warning: the writer's own attitudes fall loosely into the first (liberal) grouping, although he belongs to no political party.
5   *SE*, vol. 18, pp. 120–1.
6   J. C. Flugel, *Man, Morals and Society*, Duckworth, London, 1945, p. 283.
7   Ibid., pp. 284–96.
8   R. E. Money-Kyrle, *Psychoanalysis and Politics*, Duckworth, London, 1951, pp. 150–3.
9   R. E. Money-Kyrle, *Man's Picture of his World*, Duckworth, London, 1961, p. 180.
10 R. E. Money-Kyrle, 'Politics from the point of view of psychoanalysis', in D. Meltzer and E. O'Shaughnessy (eds), *The Collected Papers of Roger Money-Kyrle*, Clunie, Perth, 1978, p. 372.
11 D. Meltzer, *Sexual States of Mind*, Clunie, Perth, 1973, pp. 154–5.
12 H. T. Himmelweit, P. Humphreys, M. Jaeger and M. Katz, *How Voters Decide*, Academic Press, London, 1981.
13 Ibid., p. 140.
14 Ibid., p. 106.
15 *W*, vol. 3, pp. 181–2.
16 *W*, vol. 3, p. 183.
17 *W*, vol. 1, pp. 262–89.
18 H. Segal, *Introduction to the Work of Melanie Klein*, Hogarth Press, London, 1973, pp. 83–4.
19 *W*, vol. 1, pp. 344–69.
20 Segal, op.cit., pp. 95–6.
21 Conservative Party, *The Conservative Manifesto 1979*, Conservative Party, London, 1979, p. 6.
22 Labour Party, *The New Hope for Britain*, Labour Party, London, 1983, p. 17.
23 Conservative Party, *The Conservative Manifesto 1983*, Conservative Party, 1983, pp. 18–19.
24 Labour Party, op.cit., pp. 10, 29.
25 Conservative Party, op.cit., 1983, pp. 45, 31.
26 Labour Party, op.cit., pp. 23, 20, 21.
27 Conservative Party, op.cit., 1983, pp. 24–5, 28, 29.
28 Labour Party, op.cit., p. 33.
29 Conservative Party, op.cit., 1983, p. 31.

30 Flugel, op.cit., p. 298.
31 R. Skynner and J. Cleese, *Families and How to Survive Them*, Methuen, London, 1983, pp. 131–2.
32 *W*, vol. 3, p. 192.
33 *W*, vol. 3, p. 217.
34 *W*, vol. 3, p. 199.
35 *W*, vol. 3, p. 198.
36 *SE*, vol. 20, p. 253.

Index

action and observation, 26–7
adolescence, 41–2
aggregation, 9–10, 74–5, 87–8
analytical theories, 29–31
anxiety, 33–4

basic assumptions, 54–5; properties, 56–7
Bettelheim, B., 45, 49
Bion, W.R., 8, 32, 58, 77
Bion paradox, the, 77–80
Bon, G. le, 52

character traits, 125–8
collective unconscious, 7–9
conception and repression, 24–6
Conservative Party, 122, 123, 124

defence mechanisms, 27–8
depressive position, the, 36–7; in analysis, 40–1

ego, the, 20–1
Edgeworth, F.Y., 80
Einstein, A., 79
Ellis, H., 43

factory example, 68–70
Flugel, J.C., 109, 110, 125
Freud, A., 32
Freud, S., 1, 3, 4, 5, 7, 8, 9, 10, 16, 28, 29, 31, 32, 47, 49, 58, 79, 99, 100, 101, 103, 109, 128
Freudian social theory, 99–102
Fromm, E., 8, 9

greed and envy, 35–6; in political attitude, 116–19
group anxieties, 52–3
group defences, 59–61
group leaders, 55–6
group relations example, 61–5
groups, 48–50; latent and active, 75–6

Himmelweit, H.T., 114, 115
hospital example, 65–8

id, the, 19–20
identification, 53–4
individual aims, 6–7, 76
instincts, 17–19; analytical views, 31
institutions, 4–6, 77
invisible hand, the, 1–4, 102–3, 128

Jacques, E., 42, 68
Jones, E., 107

Kermode, F., 6
Klein, M., 30, 95, 117, 118, 119, 120, 126, 127

INDEX

Labour Party, 122, 123, 124
learning from experience, 28–9
left and right, 113–14; empirical views, 114–16

manifestos, 122–5
Marx, K., 9
material wants example, 90–2
Meltzer, D., 112
Menzies, I.E.P., 65
mid-life, 42–3
mind, the, 11–12; analytical views, 31–2; development, 33; a model, 12–14
Money-Kyrle, R.E., 107, 110, 111

neurotic mechanisms, 46–7

objects, 16–17
Oedipus crisis, the, 43–5
Oedipus myth, the, 45
omnipotence and manic reparation, 37–8; in political attitude, 119–22

pairing, 57–9
Pareto, V., 80
paranoid position, the, 34–5; in analysis, 38–40
phantasies, 15–16

political attitudes, 106–8; analytical views, 109–13
projection and introjection, 21–3
psychotic mechanisms, 45–6

rationality, 50–1; formalized, 70–3; group, 51–2
religions example, 88–90
Rice, A.K., 65
Russell, B., 48

Saussure, F. de, 6
Segal, H., 39, 40, 119, 120
Skynner, R. and Cleese, J., 126
Smith, A., 1
society, 4
stable institutions, 84–5; formalized, 104–5; properties, 85–7
superego, the, 23–4

tenable institutions, 80–1; formalized, 103–4; properties, 81–3
thoughts, 14–5
Trotter, W., 58

university examples, 92–9

Wisdom, J.O., 77